n or before

Marx's Das Kapital

A Biography

Current and forthcoming titles in the
Books That Changed the World series:

Marx's
Das Kapital
A Biography

FRANCIS WHEEN

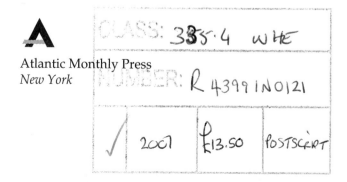

Atlantic Monthly Press
New York

First published in Great Britain in 2007 by Atlantic Books, an imprint of Grove Atlantic Ltd.

Printed in the United States of America

FIRST AMERICAN EDITION

ISBN-10: 0-87113-970-7

ISBN-13: 978-0-87113-970-2

Designed by Richard Marston

Atlantic Monthly Press
an imprint of Grove/Atlantic, Inc.
841 Broadway
New York, NY 10003

Distributed by Publishers Group West

www.groveatlantic.com

07 08 09 10 11 12   10 9 8 7 6 5 4 3 2 1

CONTENTS

A NOTE ON TRANSLATIONS

If you wish to read Marx's masterpiece for yourself, the least intimidating option is *Capital: A New Abridgement*, edited by David McLellan (OUP World's Classics), a one-volume collection of the most important chapters. Its extracts from Volume I are in the original English translation of 1887; the translations from Volume II are by McLellan himself; the material for Volume III comes from the anonymous Moscow translation published in 1971.

If you want to plunge straight into a full, unabridged version, I recommend the Penguin Classics edition in three volumes, translated by Ben Fowkes and with an introduction (which you may decide to skip) by Ernest Mandel.

Since no single translation is perfect, I have used various sources for the passages from *Das Kapital* cited in this book. Some of the quotations are from the Penguin text, some from the World's Classics, some from the *Marx & Engels Collected Works* (50 vols, Lawrence & Wishart) – and some are my own.

The Unknown Masterpiece

In February 1867, shortly before delivering the first volume of *Das Kapital* to the printers, Karl Marx urged Friedrich Engels to read *The Unknown Masterpiece* by Honoré de Balzac. The story was itself a little masterpiece, he said, 'full of the most delightful irony'.

We don't know whether Engels heeded the advice. If he did, he would certainly have spotted the irony but might have been surprised that his old friend could take any delight in it. *The Unknown Masterpiece* is the tale of Frenhofer, a great painter who spends ten years working and reworking a portrait which will revolutionize art by providing 'the most complete representation of reality'. When at last his fellow artists Poussin and Porbus are allowed to inspect the finished canvas, they are horrified to see a blizzard of random forms and colours piled one upon another in confusion. 'Ah!' Frenhofer cries, misinterpreting their wide-eyed amazement. 'You did not anticipate such perfection!' But then he overhears Poussin telling Porbus that eventually Frenhofer must discover the truth – the portrait has been overpainted so many times that nothing remains.

'Nothing on my canvas!' exclaimed Frenhofer, glancing alternately at the two painters and his picture.

'What have you done?' said Porbus in an undertone to Poussin.

The old man seized the young man's arm roughly, and said to him: 'You see nothing there, clown! varlet! miscreant! hound! Why, what brought you here, then? – My good Porbus,' he continued, turning to the older painter, 'can it be that you, you too, are mocking at me? Answer me! I am your friend; tell me, have I spoiled my picture?'

Porbus hesitated, he dared not speak; but the anxiety depicted on the old man's white face was so heart-rending that he pointed to the canvas saying: 'Look!'

Frenhofer gazed at his picture for a moment and staggered.

'Nothing! Nothing! And I have worked ten years!'

He fell upon a chair and wept.

After banishing the two men from his studio, Frenhofer burns all his paintings and kills himself.

According to Marx's son-in-law Paul Lafargue, Balzac's tale 'made a great impression on him because it was in part a description of his own feelings'. Marx had toiled for many years on his own unseen masterpiece, and throughout this long gestation his customary reply to those who asked for a glimpse of the work-in-progress was identical to that of Frenhofer: 'No, no! I have still to put some finishing touches to it. Yesterday, towards evening, I thought that it was done…

This morning, by daylight, I realized my error.' As early as 1846, when the book was already overdue, Marx wrote to his German publisher: 'I shall not have it published without revising it yet again, both as regards matter and style. It goes without saying that a writer who works continuously cannot, at the end of six months, publish word for word what he wrote six months earlier.' Twelve years later, still no nearer completion, he explained that 'the thing is proceeding very slowly because no sooner does one set about finally disposing of subjects to which one has devoted years of study than they start revealing new aspects and demand to be thought out further.' An obsessive perfectionist, he was forever seeking out new hues for his palette – studying mathematics, learning about the movement of celestial spheres, teaching himself Russian so he could read books on the country's land system. Or, to quote Frenhofer again: 'Alas! I thought for a moment that my work was finished; but I have certainly gone wrong in some details, and my mind will not be at rest until I have cleared away my doubts. I have decided to travel, and visit Turkey, Greece and Asia in search of models, in order to compare my picture with Nature in different forms.'

Why did Marx recall Balzac's tale at the very moment when he was preparing to unveil his greatest work to public scrutiny? Did he fear that he too might have laboured in vain, that his 'complete representation of reality' would prove unintelligible? He certainly had some such apprehensions – Marx's character was a curious hybrid of ferocious self-confidence and anguished self-doubt – and he tried to forestall criticism by warning in the preface that 'I assume, of course, a reader who is willing to learn something new and therefore to think for himself.' But what ought to strike us most forcibly about his identification with the creator of the unknown masterpiece is that Frenhofer is an *artist* – not a political economist, nor yet a philosopher or historian or polemicist. The most 'delightful irony' of all in *The Unknown Masterpiece*, noted by the American writer Marshall Berman, is that Balzac's account of the picture is a perfect description of a twentieth-century abstract painting – and the fact that he couldn't have known this merely deepens the resonance. 'The point is that where one age sees only chaos and incoherence, a later or more modern age may discover meaning and beauty,' Berman writes. 'Thus the very open-endedness of Marx's later work can make contact with our time in ways that more "finished" nineteenth-century work cannot: *Das Kapital* reaches beyond the well-made works of Marx's century into the discontinuous modernism of our own.' Like Frenhofer, Marx was a modernist *avant la lettre*. His famous account of dislocation in the *Communist Manifesto* – 'all that is solid melts into air' – prefigures the hollow men and the unreal city depicted by T. S. Eliot, or Yeats's 'Things fall apart; the centre cannot hold'. By the time he wrote *Das Kapital*, he was pushing out beyond conventional prose into radical literary collage – juxtaposing voices and quotations from mythology and literature, from factory inspectors' reports and fairy tales, in the manner of Ezra Pound's *Cantos* or Eliot's *The Waste Land. Das Kapital* is as discordant as Schoenberg, as nightmarish as Kafka.

Karl Marx saw himself as a creative artist, a poet of dialectic. 'Now, regarding my work, I will tell you the plain truth about it,' he wrote to Engels in July 1865. 'Whatever shortcomings they may have, the advantage of my writings is that they are an artistic whole.' It was to poets and novelists, far more than to philosophers or political essayists, that he looked for insights into people's material motives and interests: in a letter of December 1868 he copied out a passage from another work by Balzac, *The Village Priest*, and asked if Engels could confirm the picture from his own knowledge of practical economics. (The conservative, royalist Balzac may seem an unlikely hero, but Marx always held that great writers have insights into social reality that transcend their personal prejudices.) Had he wished to write a conventional economic treatise he would have done so, but his ambition was far more audacious. Berman describes the author of *Das Kapital* as 'one of the great tormented giants of the nineteenth century – alongside Beethoven, Goya, Tolstoy, Dostoevsky, Ibsen, Nietzsche, Van Gogh – who drive us crazy, as they drove themselves, but whose agony generated so much of the spiritual capital on which we still live'.

Yet how many people would think of including Karl Marx in a list of great writers and artists? Even in our post-modern era, the fractured narrative and radical discontinuity of *Das Kapital* are mistaken by many potential readers for formlessness and incomprehensibility. The main purpose of my own book is to persuade at least some of these readers to look again: anyone willing to grapple with Beethoven, Goya or

Tolstoy should be able to 'learn something new' from a reading of *Das Kapital* – not least because its subject still governs our lives. As Marshall Berman asks: how can *Das Kapital* end while capital lives on?

It is deeply fitting that Marx never finished his masterpiece. The first volume was the only one to appear in his lifetime, and the subsequent volumes were assembled by others after his death, based on notes and drafts found in his study. Marx's work is as open-ended – and thus as resilient – as the capitalist system itself. He was indeed one of the great tormented giants. Before approaching his masterpiece we must seek out the sources of Marx's torment, and of his inspiration.

CHAPTER 1

Gestation

Although *Das Kapital* is usually categorized as a work of economics, Karl Marx turned to the study of political economy only after many years of spadework in philosophy and literature. It is these intellectual foundations that underpin the project, and it is his personal experience of alienation that gives such intensity to the analysis of an economic system which estranges people from one another and from the world they inhabit – a world in which humans are enslaved by the monstrous power of inanimate capital and commodities.

Marx himself was an outsider from the moment of his birth, on 5 May 1818 – a Jewish boy in a predominantly Catholic city, Trier, within a Prussian state whose official religion was evangelical Protestantism. Although the Rhineland had been annexed by France during the Napoleonic wars, three years before his birth it was reincorporated into Imperial Prussia and the Jews of Trier thus became subject to an edict banning them from practising in the professions: Karl's father, Heinrich Marx, had to convert to Lutheranism in order to work as an attorney. No wonder the young Karl Marx began to brood upon alienation. 'We cannot always attain the position to which we believe we are called,' he wrote in a schoolboy essay, at the age of seventeen. 'Our relations in society have to some extent already begun to be established before we are in a position to determine them.'

His father encouraged Karl to read voraciously. The years of annexation had given Heinrich a taste for French flavours in politics, religion, life and art: one of his grandchildren described him as 'a real eighteenth-century "Frenchman" who knew his Voltaire and his Rousseau by heart'. The boy's other intellectual mentor was Heinrich's friend Baron Ludwig von Westphalen, a cultured and liberal government official who introduced Karl to poetry and music (and to his daughter Jenny von Westphalen, the future Mrs Karl Marx). On long walks together the Baron would recite passages from Homer and Shakespeare, which his young companion learned by heart – and later used as the essential seasonings in his own writings. In adult life Marx re-enacted those happy hikes with von Westphalen by declaiming scenes from Shakespeare, Dante and Goethe while leading his own family up to Hampstead Heath for Sunday picnics. As Professor S. S. Prawer has written, anyone in Karl Marx's household was obliged to live 'in a perpetual flurry of allusions to English literature'. There was a quotation for every occasion: to flatten a political enemy, enliven a dry text, heighten a joke, authenticate an emotion – or breathe life into an inanimate abstraction, as when capital itself speaks in the voice of Shylock (in Volume I of *Das Kapital*) to justify the exploitation of child labour in factories.

Workmen and factory inspectors protested on hygienic and moral grounds, but Capital answered:

My deeds upon my head! I crave the law,
The penalty and forfeit of my bond.

To prove that money is a radical leveller, Marx quotes a speech from *Timon of Athens* on money as the 'common whore of mankind', followed by another from Sophocles' *Antigone* ('Money! Money's the curse of man, none greater!/That's what wrecks cities, banishes men from home,/Tempts and deludes the most well-meaning soul,/Pointing out the way to infamy and shame...'). Economists with anachronistic models and categories are likened to Don Quixote, who 'paid the penalty for wrongly imagining that knight-errantry was equally compatible with all economic forms of society'.

Marx's earliest ambitions were literary. As a law student at the University of Berlin he wrote a book of poetry, a verse drama and even a novel, *Scorpion and Felix*, which was dashed off in a fit of intoxicated whimsy while under the spell of Laurence Sterne's *Tristram Shandy*. After these experiments, he admitted defeat: 'Suddenly, as if by a magic touch – oh, the touch was at first a shattering blow – I caught sight of the distant realm of true poetry like a distant fairy palace, and all my creations crumbled into nothing... A curtain had fallen, my holy of holies was rent asunder, and new gods had to be installed.' Suffering some kind of breakdown, he was ordered by his doctor to retreat to the countryside for a long rest – whereupon he at last succumbed to the siren voice of G. W. F.

Hegel, the recently deceased professor of philosophy at Berlin, whose legacy was the subject of intense dispute among fellow students and lecturers. In his youth Hegel had been an idealistic supporter of the French Revolution, but by middle age he had become comfortable and complaisant, believing that a truly mature man should recognize 'the objective necessity and reasonableness of the world as he finds it'. According to Hegel, 'All that is real is rational,' and since the Prussian state was undoubtedly real, in the sense that it existed, his conservative supporters argued that it must therefore be rational and above reproach. Those who championed his more subversive early work – the Young Hegelians – preferred to quote the second half of that dictum: 'All that is rational is real.' An absolute monarchy, buttressed by censors and secret police, was palpably irrational and therefore unreal, a mirage that would disappear as soon as anyone dared touch it.

At university, Marx 'adopted the habit of making extracts from all the books I read' – a habit he never lost. A reading list from this period shows the precocious scope of his intellectual explorations. While writing a paper on the philosophy of law he made a detailed study of Winckelmann's *History of Art*, started to teach himself English and Italian, translated Tacitus's *Germania* and Aristotle's *Rhetoric*, read Francis Bacon and 'spent a good deal of time on Reimarus, to whose book on the artistic instincts of animals I applied my mind with delight'. This is the same eclectic, omnivorous and often tangential style of research which gave *Das Kapital* its extraordinary breadth of reference. The description of Democritus in Marx's doctoral thesis, on 'The Difference Between Democritean and Epicurean Philosophy', looks remarkably like a self-portrait: 'Cicero calls him a *vir eruditus.* He is competent in physics, ethics, mathematics, in the encyclopaedic disciplines, in every art.'

For a while, Marx seemed uncertain how best to use all that erudition. After gaining his doctorate he thought of becoming a philosophy lecturer, but then decided that daily proximity to professors would be intolerable. 'Who would want to have to talk always with intellectual skunks, with people who study only for the purpose of finding new dead ends in every corner of the world!' Besides, since leaving university Marx had been turning his thoughts from idealism to materialism, from the abstract to the actual. 'Since every true philosophy is the intellectual quintessence of its time,' he wrote in 1842, 'the time must come when philosophy not only internally by its content, but also externally through its form, comes into contact and interaction with the real world of its day.' That spring he began writing for a new liberal newspaper in Cologne, the *Rheinische Zeitung;* within six months he had been appointed editor.

Marx's journalism is characterized by a reckless belligerence which explains why he spent most of his adult life in exile and political isolation. His very first article for the *Rheinische Zeitung* was a lacerating assault on both the intolerance of Prussian absolutism and the feeble-mindedness of its liberal opponents. Not content with making enemies of the government and opposition simultaneously, he turned against his own comrades as well, denouncing the Young Hegelians for 'rowdiness and blackguardism'. Only two months after Marx's assumption of editorial responsibility, the provincial governor asked the censorship ministers in Berlin to prosecute him for 'impudent and disrespectful criticism'. No less a figure than Tsar Nicholas of Russia also begged the Prussian king to suppress the *Rheinische Zeitung*, having taken umbrage at an anti-Russian diatribe. The paper was duly closed in March 1843: at the age of twenty-four, Marx was already wielding a pen that could terrify and infuriate the crowned heads of Europe. Realizing that he had no future in Prussia, he accepted an invitation to move to Paris as co-editor of a new journal-in-exile for Germans, the *Deutsche-Französische Jahrbücher*. There was only one caveat: 'I am engaged to be married and I cannot, must not and will not leave Germany without my fiancée.'

Karl Marx married Jenny von Westphalen in June 1843. For the rest of the summer, while awaiting their summons to Paris, he and his new bride enjoyed an extended honeymoon in the fashionable spa resort of Kreuznach. When not walking by the river he shut himself away in a workroom, reading and writing with furious intensity. Marx always liked to work out his ideas on paper, and a surviving page from the Kreuznach notebooks shows the process in action:

Note. Under Louis XVIII, the constitution by grace of the king (Charter imposed by the king); under Louis Philippe, the king

by grace of the constitution (imposed kingship). In general
we can note that the conversion of the subject into the
predicate, and of the predicate into the subject, the exchange
of that which determines for that which is determined, is
always the most immediate revolution… The king makes the
law (old monarchy), the law makes the king (new monarchy).

This simple grammatical inversion also disclosed the flaw in
German philosophy. Hegel had assumed that 'the Idea of the
State' was the subject, with society as its object, whereas history
showed the opposite. Turn Hegel upside down and the
problem was solved: religion does not make man, man makes
religion; the constitution does not create the people, but the
people create the constitution. Although he took the idea
from Ludwig Feuerbach, who in a recent book had argued
that 'thought arises from being, not being from thought',
Marx extended its logic from abstract philosophy to the material
world. As he wrote in his *Theses on Feuerbach*, published in
1845, 'The philosophers have only *interpreted* the world, in
various ways; the point is to *change* it.' Here, still in the womb,
is the essential thesis of *Das Kapital*. However glorious its
apparent economic triumphs, capitalism remains a disaster
since it turns people into commodities, exchangeable for
other commodities. Until humans can assert themselves as
the subjects of history rather than its objects, there is no escape
from this tyranny.

The presiding triumvirate of the *Deutsche-Französische
Jahrbücher* – Karl Marx, the journalist Arnold Ruge, the poet

Georg Herwegh – arrived in Paris in the autumn of 1843 and set up a 'phalanstery' or commune in the Rue Vanneau, inspired by the utopian ideas of the French socialist Charles Fourier. The experiment in communal living was short-lived, as was the journal itself: only one issue appeared before the editors fell out. Marx then took up an offer to write for *Vorwärts*, a bi-weekly Communist newspaper published by German exiles, in which he first outlined his conviction that class consciousness was the fertilizer of revolution. 'The German proletariat is the theoretician of the European proletariat, just as the English proletariat is its economist, and the French proletariat its politician,' he wrote, prefiguring a later assessment by Engels that Marxism itself was a hybrid of these three bloodlines. Marx was already well versed in German philosophy and French politics; now he set about educating himself in British economics, reading his way systematically through the works of Adam Smith, David Ricardo and James Mill, scribbling a running commentary as he went along. These notes, commonly known as the Paris manuscripts, are an early rough draft of what eventually became *Das Kapital*.

The first manuscript begins with this straightforward assertion: 'Wages are determined by the fierce struggle between capitalist and worker. The capitalist inevitably wins. The capitalist can live longer without the worker than the worker can without him.' If capital is nothing more than the accumulated fruits of the worker's labour, then a country's capitals and revenues grow only when 'more and more of the worker's products are being taken from him, when his own labour increasingly confronts him as alien property and the means of his existence and of his activity are increasingly concentrated in the hands of the capitalist'. Even in the most propitious economic conditions, the worker's fate is inevitably 'overwork and early death, reduction to a machine, enslavement to capital'. His labour becomes an external being which 'exists outside him, independently of him and alien to him, and begins to confront him as an autonomous power; the life which he has bestowed on the object confronts him as hostile and alien'. This image comes from one of Marx's favourite books, *Frankenstein*, the tale of a monster that turns against its creator. Although some scholars claim that there is a 'radical break' between the thought of the young Marx and the mature Marx, both the analysis and its ghoulish expression are manifestly the work of the same man who argued in *Das Kapital*, more than twenty years later, that the means by which capitalism raises its productivity 'distort the worker into a fragment of a man, they degrade him to the level of a machine, they destroy the actual content of his labour by turning it into a torment; they alienate from him the intellectual potentialities of the labour process... they transform his lifetime into working time, and drag his wife and child beneath the juggernaut of capital'.

In August 1844, while Jenny Marx was visiting her mother in Trier, the twenty-three-year-old Friedrich Engels came to call on Karl at his Parisian apartment. They had met once before, fleetingly, at the office of the *Rheinische Zeitung*, and more recently Marx had been profoundly impressed by a 'Critique of Political Economy' which Engels submitted to the *Deutsche-Französische Jahrbücher*. One can see why: though he now believed that social and economic forces drove the engine of history, he had no direct knowledge of capitalism in practice. Engels was well placed to enlighten him, as the son and heir of a German cotton manufacturer who owned mills in Manchester – heartland of the Industrial Revolution and birthplace of the Anti-Corn Law League, a city teeming with Chartists, Owenists and socialist agitators of every kind. Engels had moved to Lancashire in the autumn of 1842, ostensibly to learn about the family business but actually with the intention of observing the human consequences of Victorian capitalism. By day he was a diligent young manager at the Cotton Exchange; after hours he changed sides, exploring the city's proletarian streets and slums to gather material for his early masterpiece, *The Condition of the Working Class in England* (1845).

Although Marx and Engels spent ten days together in Paris, the only account of their epic conversation comes in a single sentence written by Engels more than forty years later: 'When I visited Marx in Paris in the summer of 1844, our complete agreement in all theoretical fields became evident and our joint work dates from that time.' They complemented each other perfectly – Marx with his wealth of knowledge, Engels with his knowledge of wealth. Marx wrote slowly and painfully, with countless inky deletions and emendations, while Engels's manuscripts are neat, businesslike and elegant. Marx lived in chaos and penury for most of his life; Engels held down a full-time job while also maintaining a formidable output of books, letters and journalism – and still found the time to enjoy the pleasures of high bourgeois life, with horses in his stables and plenty of wine in his cellars. Yet despite his obvious advantages, Engels knew from the outset that he would never be the dominant partner. He accepted, without complaint or jealousy, that his duty was to give the intellectual and financial support that made Marx's work possible. 'I simply cannot understand,' he wrote, 'how anyone can be envious of genius; it's something so very special that we who have not got it know it to be unattainable right from the start; but to be envious of anything like that one must have to be frightfully small-minded.'

They had no secrets from each other, no taboos: their correspondence is a pungent stew of history and gossip, arcane economics and schoolboy jokes. Engels also served as a kind of substitute mother to Marx – despatching pocket money, fussing over his health and continually warning him not to neglect his studies. In the earliest surviving letter, from October 1844, he was already urging Marx to turn his political and economic notes into a book without delay: 'See to it that the material you've collected is soon launched into the world. It's high time, heaven knows!' Three months later his impatience was growing: 'Do try and finish your political economy book, even if there's much in it that you yourself are dissatisfied with, it doesn't really matter; minds are ripe and we must strike while the iron's hot… So try and finish *before* April, do as I do, set yourself a date by which you will *definitely have finished,* and make sure it gets into print quickly.' A forlorn hope: more than two decades passed before the first volume of *Das Kapital* was at last delivered to the presses.

Engels himself is not entirely blameless here. Soon after meeting Marx in Paris he proposed that they collaborate on a short pamphlet – forty pages at most – criticizing the more excitable Young Hegelians. Having finished his own portion of twenty pages within a few days, Engels was 'not a little surprised' several months later to learn that the pamphlet had now swollen to 300 pages. Marx was the kind of writer who could never resist a distraction, preferring the immediate gratification of pamphlets and articles to the mute inglorious toil required for his *magnum opus,* then provisionally titled *A Critique of Economics and Politics.* Despite having promised to deliver the economic manuscript to the German publisher Karl Leske by the end of summer 1845, he set it aside after writing no more than a table of contents. 'It seemed to me very important,' he explained to Leske, 'to *precede* my *positive* development with a polemical piece against German philosophy and German socialism up till the present. This is necessary in order to prepare the public for the viewpoint adopted in my Economy, which is diametrically opposed to German scholarship past and present... If need be, I could produce numerous letters I have received from Germany and France as proof that this work is most eagerly awaited by the public.' A likely story: the book in question, *The German Ideology,* didn't find a publisher until 1932. 'We abandoned the manuscript to the gnawing criticism of the mice,' Marx wrote, 'all the more willingly as we had achieved our main purpose – self-clarification.'

Yet he was still unable or unwilling to give the economic work his full attention. There would be many more polemical interruptions over the next few years: *The Poverty of Philosophy*, a 100-page philippic against Pierre-Joseph Proudhon; *The Great Men of the Exile*, a verbose satire on the 'more noteworthy jackasses' and 'democratic scallywags' of the socialist diaspora; *The Secret Diplomatic History of the Eighteenth Century*, an anti-Russian tirade; *The Story of the Life of Lord Palmerston*, in which he sought to prove that the British foreign secretary was a secret agent of the Russian Tsar; and *Herr Vogt*, a flailing assault on the professor of natural science at Berne University, who had incurred Marx's wrath by calling him a charlatan and a sponger. 'Tit for tat, reprisals make the world go round,' he hummed merrily to himself while wasting the better part of a year on his feud with Vogt.

Progress was further hampered by continual domestic upheavals. In January 1845 the Prussian envoy in Paris protested to King Louis Philippe about an article from *Vorwärts* in which Marx ridiculed King Friedrich Wilhelm IV. The French Interior Minister duly closed the magazine and ordered the author's expulsion from France. The only king in mainland Europe willing to take him in was Leopold I of Belgium, and then only after receiving a written promise that Marx would not publish 'any work on current politics'. Assuming that this needn't prevent him from *participating* in politics, Marx summoned Engels to join him in Brussels, where they founded a Communist Correspondence Committee to maintain 'a continuous interchange of letters' with socialist groups in Western Europe. By 1847 the committee had converted itself into a branch of the newly formed Communist League in London, which then invited Marx to produce a draft statement of principles. What he gave them was *The Manifesto of the Communist Party*, probably the most widely read and influential pamphlet in history.

When he wrote the manifesto, in the first weeks of 1848, Marx thought that bourgeois capitalism had already served its purpose and would soon be buried under its own contradictions. By driving hitherto isolated workers into mills and factories, modern industry had created the very conditions in which the proletariat could combine into an irresistible force. 'What the bourgeoisie, therefore, produces, above all, is its own grave-diggers.' Because he thought he was rehearsing a funeral oration, however, he could afford to be generous to the vanquished foe. One critic has described the manifesto as 'a lyrical celebration of bourgeois works', and first-time readers are often astonished by the praise he lavishes on the enemy:

> The bourgeoisie, historically, has played a most
> revolutionary part. The bourgeoisie, wherever it has got the
> upper hand, has put an end to all feudal, patriarchal, idyllic
> relations. It has pitilessly torn asunder the motley feudal
> ties that bound man to his 'natural superiors', and has left

remaining no other nexus between man and man than naked self-interest, than callous 'cash payment'. It has drowned the most heavenly ecstasies of religious fervour, of chivalrous enthusiasm, of philistine sentimentalism, in the icy water of egotistical calculation. It has resolved personal worth into exchange-value... The bourgeoisie cannot exist without revolutionizing the instruments of production, and thereby the relations of production, and with them the whole relations of society.

He would replay these themes with far greater depth and complexity in *Das Kapital*, but for now there was no time to elaborate. Both the manifesto's opening sentence ('A spectre is haunting Europe – the spectre of Communism') and its equally famous conclusion ('Let the ruling classes tremble at a communistic revolution... WORKING MEN OF ALL COUN-TRIES, UNITE!') confirm that this is a piece of agitprop, albeit one of unmatched intelligence, written in haste at a time when insurrection seemed imminent.

By happy coincidence, revolution did indeed break out in the week of its publication in February 1848, first in Paris and then, with the speed of brushfire, across much of continental Europe. Following the abdication of King Louis Philippe and the proclamation of a French Republic, the panic-stricken Belgian government ordered Karl Marx to quit the country within twenty-four hours and never return. Fortunately he had just received an invitation from the new provisional gov-ernment in Paris: 'Good and loyal Marx... Tyranny exiled you, now free France opens its doors to you and all those who are fighting for the holy cause, the fraternal cause of all peoples.' After only a month in Paris, however, he departed for Cologne in the hope of spreading revolution in Germany. His chosen weapon, as so often, was the printed word: he established a new daily newspaper, the *Neue Rheinische Zeitung*, which endured constant official harassment throughout its brief life. In July he was hauled up before the magistrates for 'insulting or libelling the chief prosecutor'; in September, after the declaration of martial law, the Cologne military commander suspended publication for a month; the following February, when any possibility of revolution had been thoroughly extinguished, he was charged with 'incitement to revolt' but persuaded the jury to acquit him with a brilliant speech from the dock. Finally, in May 1849 the Prussian authorities prosecuted half of the editorial staff and recommended the other half – including Marx, who had forfeited his citizenship – for deportation.

He returned to Paris in June 1849, only to find the city in the grip of a royalist reaction and a cholera epidemic. Served with an official order banishing him to the malaria-infested *département* of Morbihan in Brittany, he took refuge in the only European country still willing to accommodate rootless revolutionaries. He sailed to Britain on 27 August 1849 and remained there until his death in 1883. 'You must leave for London at once,' he wrote to Engels, who was visiting Switzerland. 'In London we shall get down to business.'

A few months after his arrival in London, Karl Marx

noticed a working model of an electric railway engine in the window of a Regent Street shop. He became 'flushed and excited', according to a witness – not from the thrill of novelty but because of the economic implications. 'The problem is solved – the consequences are indefinable,' he told his fellow gawpers. 'In the wake of the economic revolution the political must necessarily follow, for the latter is only the expression of the former.' It seems unlikely that anyone else in the Regent Street throng had paused to consider the economic and political consequences of this Trojan iron horse; for Marx, it was all that mattered.

Having obtained a ticket to the British Museum reading room in June 1850, he spent much of the next year reading books on economics and back numbers of *The Economist.* By April 1851 he claimed to be 'so far advanced that I will have finished the whole economic stuff in five weeks' time. And having done that, I shall complete the political economy at home and apply myself to another branch of learning at the Museum.' He sat in the reading room from nine in the morning until seven in the evening most days, but there seemed no end to the task he had set himself. 'The material I am working on is so damnably involved that, no matter how I exert myself, I shall not finish for another six to eight weeks,' he wrote in June. 'There are, moreover, constant interruptions of a practical kind, inevitable in the wretched circumstances in which we are vegetating here...'

From the moment of their arrival in London, Karl and Jenny Marx were beset by one domestic crisis after another.

They already had three young children, and a fourth was born in November 1849. Evicted from a Chelsea flat in May 1850 for non-payment of rent, they found temporary shelter in the house of a Jewish lace-dealer in Dean Street, Soho, where they spent a miserable summer teetering on the edge of destitution before moving to a more permanent billet up the road. Jenny was pregnant again, and constantly ill. Engels came to the rescue by sacrificing his own journalistic ambitions in London and returning to the Manchester office of Ermen & Engels, where he remained for the next twenty years. Although this was largely for the purpose of supporting his brilliant, impecunious friend, he also acted as a kind of agent behind enemy lines, sending Marx confidential details of the cotton trade and expert observations on the state of international markets – as well as regular consignments of banknotes, pilfered from the petty-cash box or guilefully prised out of the company's bank account.

Even with these subventions, the Marxes lived in squalor and near despair. The furniture and fittings in their two-room apartment were all broken, tattered or torn, with a thick carpet of dust over everything. The entire ménage – parents, children, housekeeper – slept in a small back bedroom, while the other room served as a study, playroom and kitchen. A Prussian police spy who inveigled his way into the flat reported back to his masters in Berlin that Marx 'leads the existence of a real bohemian intellectual… Though he is often idle for days on end, he will work day and night with tireless endurance when he has a great deal of work to do. He has no fixed times for going to sleep and waking up. He often stays up all night, and then lies down fully clothed on the sofa at midday and sleeps till evening, untroubled by the comings and goings of the whole world.' This chaotic existence was punctuated by regular domestic tragedies. The Marxes' youngest son, Guido, died suddenly from a fit of convulsions in November 1850; their one-year-old daughter Franziska died at Easter 1852 after a severe attack of bronchitis. Another son, his beloved Edgar, died of consumption in March 1855. Out of his wits with grief, Marx stepped forward as the coffin was lowered into the earth and convinced most of the mourners that he intended to hurl himself in after it. One stuck out a restraining hand, just in case.

'If only,' Engels wrote in his letter of condolence after Franziska's death, 'there were some means by which you and your family could move into a more salubrious district and more spacious lodgings.' Whether or not penury killed Franziska, it certainly dominated the lives of her parents. Irate creditors – butchers, bakers, bailiffs – were continually banging at the front door and demanding payment. 'A week ago I reached the pleasant point where I am unable to go out for want of the coats I have in pawn,' Marx wrote in February 1852, 'and can no longer eat meat for want of credit.' Later that year he revealed to Engels that 'for the past eight to ten days I have been feeding the family solely on bread and potatoes, but whether I shall be able to get hold of any today is doubtful… How am I to get out of this infernal mess?' By then he was earning a regular stipend as European correspondent of the *New York Daily Tribune,* to which he submitted two articles a week at £2 apiece, but even with Engels's extra subsidy it was not enough – and, of course, provided yet another reason for failing to concentrate on his economic masterwork.

'But, for all that, the thing is rapidly approaching completion,' he wrote in June 1851. 'There comes a time when one has forcibly to break off.' This shows a comical lack of self-knowledge: Marx could happily break off from friends and political associations, but he had no such facility for letting go of his work – especially not *this* work, a vast compendium of statistics and history and philosophy which would at last lay bare the shameful secrets of capitalism. The more he researched and wrote, the further it seemed to be from completion. 'The main thing,' Engels advised in November 1851, 'is that you should once again make a public debut with a big book... It's absolutely essential to break the spell created by your prolonged absence from the German book market.' Then the project was laid aside once again, a victim of yet more 'constant interruptions'. Immediately after the French coup of December 1851 he wrote *The Eighteenth Brumaire of Louis Bonaparte* at the request of the new American weekly *Die Revolution.* The next few years were largely wasted on feuds and score-settling polemics against fellow émigrés. Marx argued that these were essential political interventions rather than manifestations of pique, since false socialist messiahs – if left unexposed – were far more attractive to the masses than genuine monarchs. 'I am engaged in a fight to the death with the sham liberals,' he declared.

What eventually drove him back to economic studies was the apparent arrival of the long-awaited international financial cataclysm in the autumn of 1857. Beginning with a bank collapse in New York, the crisis spread through Austria, Germany, France and England like a galloping apocalypse. Engels, who had been convalescing from illness, scuttled back to his post in Manchester to witness the fun – plummeting prices, daily bankruptcies and wild panic. 'The general appearance of the [Cotton] Exchange here was truly delightful,' he reported. 'The fellows are utterly infuriated by my sudden and inexplicable onset of high spirits.' Marx, too, was infected by the melodramatic spirit of the moment. Throughout the winter of 1857–8 he sat in his study until about 4 a.m. every night, collating his economic papers 'so that I at least get the outlines clear before the *déluge*'. The flood never came; but Marx continued to build his ark, convinced that it would be needed sooner or later. When his rudimentary arithmetic proved inadequate for complex economic formulae he took a quick revision course in algebra, explaining that 'for the benefit of the public it is absolutely essential to go into the matter thoroughly'.

His nocturnal scribblings, which ran to more than 800 pages, remained unseen until the Marx–Engels Institute in Moscow released them from the archives in 1939, and became widely available only with the publication of a German edition in 1953, *Grundrisse der Kritik der Politischen Oekonomie* ('Outlines of a Critique of Political Economy'). Despite its vast length, the *Grundrisse* is a fragmentary work – described by

Marx himself as a real hotchpotch – but as the missing link between the Paris manuscripts of 1844 and the first volume of *Das Kapital* (1867) it demonstrates the continuity of his ideas. There are long sections on alienation, dialectics and the meaning of money which echo passages from the 1844 manuscripts, the most striking difference being that he now merges philosophy and economics whereas before they were treated as separate disciplines. (As the German writer Ferdinand Lassalle commented, he was 'a Hegel turned economist, a Ricardo turned socialist'.) Elsewhere, the analysis of labour-power and surplus value reads like a draft of the fuller exposition of these theories in *Das Kapital.*

Marx often referred to his work in this period as 'the economic shit', and in that contemptuous phrase there was undoubtedly an element of guilt. As long ago as 1845 he had pretended that the treatise on political economy was almost finished, and over the next thirteen years he had repeated and embellished the lie so often that his friends' expectations were raised to an almost impossible pitch. Judging by the time taken, they assumed that it must indeed be a huge explosive charge that would instantly destroy the baseless edifices of capitalism. The regular bulletins to Engels in Manchester maintained the myth of striding progress. 'I have completely demolished the theory of profit as hitherto propounded,' he announced jubilantly in January 1858. In truth, however, all he had to show for those long days in the British Museum and even longer nights at his desk was a tottering pile of unpublishable notebooks, filled with random jottings.

At the beginning of 1858, Ferdinand Lassalle offered to arrange a contract for Marx with a Berlin publisher called Duncker (whose wife happened to be one of Lassalle's mistresses). Marx informed the publisher that his 'critical exposé of the system of bourgeois economy' would be divided into six books, which should be issued in instalments: '1. On Capital (contains a few introductory chapters). 2. On Landed Property. 3. On Wage Labour. 4. On the State. 5. International Trade. 6. World Market.' The first volume would be ready for the printers in May, followed by the second within a few months, and so on. However, as so often when he faced tight deadlines, Marx's body rebelled in protest. 'I've been so ill with my bilious complaint this week that I am incapable of thinking, reading, writing or, indeed, of anything,' he confided to Engels in April 1858. Beset by liver pains, he found that whenever he sat and wrote for a couple of hours 'I have to lie quite fallow for a couple of days'.

It was a familiar lament. 'Alas, we are so used to these excuses for non-completion of the work,' Engels commented many years later, when rereading some old letters. As Marx himself admitted, 'my sickness always originates in the mind'. But other distractions were real enough: his daughter Eleanor went down with whooping cough; his wife was 'a nervous wreck'; the pawnbroker and the tallyman were clamouring for payment. As Marx joked grimly, 'I don't suppose anyone has ever written about "money" when so short of the stuff.' Despite writing almost nothing through the summer, he promised at the end of September 1858 that the manuscript would be ready for posting 'in two weeks' – but confessed a month later that 'it will be weeks before I am able to send it'. Everything conspired against him: even the world economic crisis, by fizzling out too soon, had provoked a bad temper and thus given him 'the most appalling toothache'.

By the middle of November, six months after the initial deadline, Lassalle gently inquired on behalf of the Berlin publisher if the book was nearly ready. Marx replied that the procrastination 'merely signified the endeavour to give him the best value for his money'. As he explained:

> The style of everything I wrote seemed tainted with liver trouble. And I have a twofold motive for not allowing this work to be spoiled on medical grounds:
>
> It is the product of fifteen years of research, i.e. the best years of my life.
>
> In it an important view of social relations is scientifically expounded for the first time. Hence I owe it to the Party that the thing shouldn't be disfigured by the kind of heavy, wooden style proper to a disordered liver…
>
> I shall have finished about four weeks from now, having only just begun the actual writing.

This must have come as a surprise to Lassalle, who had been assured back in February that the text was in its 'final stages'. Engels, too, was in for a shock. After finally sending the parcel to Berlin in January 1859, Marx told him: 'The manuscript amounts to about twelve sheets [192 pages] of print (three instalments) and – don't be bowled over by this – although entitled "Capital in General", these instalments contain nothing as yet on the subject of capital.' After all those loud and lengthy fanfares, he had produced nothing more than a slim volume. Half of it was simply a summary of other economists' theories, and the only section of lasting interest was an autobiographical preface describing how his reading of Hegel and his journalism at the *Rheinische Zeitung* had led him to the conclusion that 'the anatomy of civil society is to be found in political economy'.

Marx put on a brave show of hyperbolic huckstering as publication day loomed, predicting that the book – now titled *A Contribution to the Critique of Political Economy* – would be translated and admired throughout the civilized world. But his friends were appalled: the German socialist Wilhelm Liebknecht said that never had a book disappointed him so much. There were few reviews. 'The secret hopes we had long nourished in regard to Karl's book were all set at naught by the Germans' conspiracy of silence,' Jenny Marx complained. 'The second instalment may startle the slugabeds out of their lethargy.'

The next instalment was due a few months after the first. Marx now adjusted the deadline slightly, imposing an 'extreme limit' of December 1859 for completing his thesis on capital, which had been so inexplicably omitted from the *Critique.* But for the next year his economic notebooks lay unopened on the desk as he pursued his feud with Karl Vogt of Berne University through newspaper articles, libel actions and a full-length book. No sooner was that finished than the new Prussian king celebrated his coronation with an amnesty for political émigrés, raising Marx's hope that he could return home and found a newspaper modelled on the *Neue Rheinische Zeitung*. This prompted a long – and fruitless – fund-raising trip to Germany in the spring of 1861, financed by Ferdinand Lassalle, followed by a return of hospitality when Lassalle decided to come to London for the second Great Exhibition in 1862. 'The fellow has wasted my time,' Marx grumbled during the third week of that ordeal, 'and, what is more, the dolt opined that, since I was not engaged upon any "business" just now, but merely upon a "theoretical work", I might just as well kill time with him!'

Lassalle's sneer at 'theory' turned out to be the goad Marx needed to finish the job which had been so calamitously interrupted by the duel with Vogt. With few journalistic commissions to divert him, he took refuge again in the British Museum reading room, gathering the ammunition for his final assault on capitalism. The notes he took in 1862 and 1863 filled more than 1,500 pages. 'I am expanding this volume,' he explained, 'since those German scoundrels estimate the value of a book in terms of its cubic capacity.' Theoretical problems which had hitherto defeated him were now as clear and invigorating as a glass of gin. Take the question of agricultural rents – or the 'shitty rent business', as he called it. 'I had long harboured misgivings as to the absolute correctness of Ricardo's theory, and have at length got to the bottom of the swindle.' David Ricardo had simply confused value and cost-price. The prices of agricultural products were higher than their actual value (as measured by the labour-time embedded in them), and the landlord pocketed the difference in the form of higher rent; but under a socialist system this surplus would be redistributed for the benefit of the workers. Even if the market price remained the same, the value of the goods – their 'social character' – would change utterly.

Marx's delight at his progress bred over-optimism. At the end of 1862 an admirer from Hanover, Dr Ludwig Kugelmann, wrote to ask when the sequel to *A Contribution to the Critique of Political Economy* could be expected. 'The second part has now at last been finished,' Marx replied, 'save for the fair copy and the final polishing before it goes to press.' He also revealed for the first time that the cumbersome working title, 'A Contribution to the Critique of Political Economy, Volume II', had been abandoned. By some inverse logic, big books deserved short names, and so 'it will appear on its own under the title *Das Kapital*'.

In truth, much more carpentry would be required before his raw timber was ready for 'final polishing'; and soon a new distraction lured him from his workshop. Marx had declined all requests to participate in new political groups ever since the collapse of the Communist League in 1850, 'firmly convinced that my theoretical studies were of greater use to the working class than my meddling with associations which had now had their day', but in September 1864 curiosity got the better of him when an invitation arrived to the inaugural meeting of the International Working Men's Association, an

Anglo-French alliance of trade unionists and socialists. Although he attended only as a silent observer, at the end of the evening he was co-opted on to the General Council – and by 1865 had become its *de facto* leader.

It was a time-consuming commitment. A letter to Engels in March 1865 describes a typical week's work: Tuesday evening was given over to the General Council, which bickered until after midnight; the next day there was a public meeting in Covent Garden to mark the anniversary of the Polish insurrection; Saturday and Monday were devoted to committee meetings on 'the French question', both of which continued until one in the morning; and so to Tuesday, with another long slanging-match between English and French members of the General Council. In between all these engagements, there were 'people dashing this way and that to see me' in connection with a conference on suffrage which was to be held the following weekend. 'What a waste of time!' he groaned. Engels thought so too. Why did his friend wish to spend hours signing membership cards and arguing with fractious committee men when he could be at his desk writing *Das Kapital*? 'I have always thought that the naïve *fraternité* in the International Association would not last long,' he warned after yet another bout of internecine squabbling among the French. 'It will pass through many more such phases and will take up a great deal of your time.'

Through the summer of 1865 Marx was vomiting every day ('in consequence of the hot weather and related biliousness') and plagued by carbuncles. A sudden influx of house guests – Jenny's brother from Germany, Marx's brother-in-law from South Africa, a niece from Maastricht – provided further unwelcome interruptions. There was also the familiar queue of creditors 'hammering on my door, becoming more and more unendurable every day'. And yet, at the still point of this whirlwind, his unknown masterpiece was nearing completion. By the end of the year *Das Kapital* was a manuscript of 1,200 pages, a blotted mess of crossings-out and indecipherable squiggles. On New Year's Day 1866 he sat down to make a fair copy, 'licking the infant clean after long birth pangs'. It took just over a year. Even liver trouble and carbuncles couldn't thwart him: he wrote the last few pages standing at his desk when an eruption of boils on the bottom made sitting too painful. (Arsenic, the usual anaesthetic, 'dulls my mind too much and I needed to keep my wits about me'.) Engels's experienced eye immediately spotted certain passages in the text where the carbuncles had left their mark, and Marx agreed that they might have given the prose a rather livid hue. 'At all events, I hope the bourgeoisie will remember my carbuncles until their dying day,' he cursed. 'What swine they are!'

The boils disappeared as soon as he completed the last page. 'I always had the feeling,' Engels told him, 'that that damn book, which you have been carrying for so long, was at the bottom of your misfortune, and you would and could never extricate yourself until you had got it off your back.' Feeling 'as voraciously fit as 500 hogs', Marx set off for Hamburg in April 1867 to deliver the manuscript and oversee its printing. Even the news that the publisher expected the next two volumes before the end of the year couldn't dampen his high spirits. 'I hope and confidently believe that in the space of a year I shall be made,' he predicted. The reactions of those who were allowed to glimpse parts of the work encouraged him to hope that his name and fame would resound throughout Europe. In the words of Johann Georg Eccarius, an old ally from the Communist League and the International Working Men's Association: 'The Prophet himself is just now having the quintessence of all wisdom published.'

CHAPTER 2

Birth

'Beginnings are always difficult in all sciences,' Marx warned in *Das Kapital's* preface. But not half as difficult as endings, he might have added: the first volume was the only one he completed before his death. The years of toil and struggle had left him physically and mentally exhausted.

'You must not wait for the second volume,' he wrote to his Russian translator in October 1868, 'the publication of which will be delayed by perhaps another six months. I cannot finish it until certain official inquiries, instituted during the last year (and 1866) in France, the United States and England, have been completed and published.' By 1870 he had a new excuse for delay: 'I was not only held up by my illness throughout the winter, I found it necessary to mug up on my Russian, because, in dealing with the land question, it has become essential to study Russian land-owning relationships from primary sources.' Over the next few years he accumulated a mountainous archive of Russian books and statistics – much to the irritation of Engels, who said he would have liked to burn the lot. He suspected Marx of using them as a barricade behind which he could hide from the exasperated appeals of his friends and publishers.

The suspicion was fully justified. When Engels began to assemble the next volume from the paper mountain left after Marx's death in 1883, he described the scale of his task in a letter to the German socialist August Bebel:

> Alongside parts that have been completely finished are others that are merely sketched out, the whole being a draft with the exception of perhaps two chapters. Quotations from sources in no kind of order, piles of them jumbled together, collected simply with a view to future selection. Besides that there is the handwriting which certainly cannot be deciphered by anyone except me, and then only with difficulty. You ask why I of all people should not have known how far the thing had got. It is quite simple: had I known, I should have pestered him night and day until it was all finished and printed. And Marx knew that better than anyone else.

The second volume appeared in 1885, followed by a third (also compiled by Engels) in 1894. What is often called the 'fourth volume', *Theories of Surplus Value* (1905), was edited by Karl Kautsky from the notes made by Marx in the mid-1860s on the history of economics, largely composed of extracts from previous theorists such as Adam Smith and David Ricardo.

In short, *Das Kapital* is an incomplete, fragmentary work: Marx's original plan, it will be recalled, envisaged six volumes. In the words of the Marxian scholar Maximilien Rubel, 'we do not have before us a Marxist bible of eternally codified canons'. One has to emphasize this because many Communists came to treat it as holy writ, maintaining that whatever Marx said was true and whatever he didn't say was not true. Both contentions are insupportable: there are silences and omissions which might have been filled had he energy enough and time; and there are errors and misconceptions, seized upon triumphantly by his critics, which should also be acknowledged by those who admire *Das Kapital*. 'The fact that Marx brilliantly discovered a new continent,' the economist Michael Lebowitz points out, 'does not mean that he correctly mapped it all.'

The *terra incognita* which he set out to explore was the new world of industrial capitalism – a landscape unknown to Adam Smith – and from the outset Marx warned readers that they were entering a fantasy land where nothing is as it seems. Look at his choice of verbs in the very first sentence of *Das Kapital*: 'The wealth of societies in which the capitalist mode of production prevails *appears as* an "immense collection of commodities"; the individual commodity *appears as* its elementary form.' (My emphasis.) Though less dramatic than the famous opening sentence of the *Communist Manifesto* ('A spectre is haunting Europe...'), it makes a similar point: we are entering a world of spectres and apparitions. The pages of *Das Kapital* are peppered with phrases such as 'phantom-like objectivity', 'unsubstantial ghost', 'pure illusion' and 'false semblance'. Only by penetrating the veils of illusion can he reveal the exploitation by which capitalism lives.

The commodity, Marx argues, has two properties: use-value and exchange-value. The usefulness of an object is obvious enough: a coat keeps us warm and dry, a loaf of bread feeds us. If exchange-value were a measure of usefulness, the loaf of bread would command a far higher price than, say, a brightly patterned silk waistcoat, which is clearly not the case. How, then, is exchange-value established?

> Let us now take two commodities, for example corn and iron. Whatever their exchange relation may be, it can always be represented by an equation in which a given quantity of corn is equated to some quantity of iron, for instance 1 quarter of corn = x cwt of iron. What does this equation signify? It signifies that a common element of identical magnitude exists in two different things, in 1 quarter of corn and similarly in x cwt of iron. Both are therefore equal to a third thing, which in itself is neither the one nor the other. Each of them, so far as it is exchange-value, must therefore be reducible to this third thing.

The one common element shared by commodities is that they are the products of labour. Therefore the value of an object must reflect the amount of labour 'congealed' in it – the labour directly involved in making the object, as well as the labour which produced the machines used in manufacture and the labour expended on acquiring the raw materials. (Marx is quick to add that he means 'socially necessary labour-time' – that is, the hours it would take an average worker to complete the job. Otherwise one might infer that a commodity made by clumsy or lazy workers would be more valuable, since they would take longer to produce it.)

So far, so conventional: similar 'labour theories of value' had been proposed by Adam Smith, David Ricardo and many other classical economists. Smith began his *Wealth of Nations* with this assertion: 'The annual labour of every nation is the fund which originally supplies it with all the necessaries and conveniences of life...' But Marx goes further. Just as commodities have a dual character, possessing both use-value and exchange-value, so labour itself has a twofold nature. Use-value is created by 'concrete' or 'useful' labour, defined by Marx as 'productive activity of a definite kind, carried on with a definite aim', whereas exchange-value derives from 'abstract' or 'undifferentiated' labour, which is measured purely in terms of its duration – and there is an inherent tension between the two. A tailor, for instance, may strive to make the hardest-wearing coat of which he or she is capable. If it is too hard-wearing, however, the purchaser need never return to buy a replacement, so jeopardizing the tailor's business. The same applies to the weaver who created the cloth from which the coat was sewn. The need to create use-value thus finds itself in conflict with the need to continue creating exchange-value.

To illustrate the two aspects of labour, Marx plunges into a lengthy and increasingly surreal meditation on the relative values of a coat and twenty yards of linen. 'Within its value relation to the linen,' he writes, 'the coat signifies more than it does outside it, just as some men count for more when inside a gold-braided uniform than they do otherwise.' As a use-value, the linen is something palpably different from the coat; as value, however, it is effectively the same thing, an expression of abstract labour. 'Thus the linen acquires a value-form different from its natural form. Its existence as value is manifested in its equality with the coat, just as the sheep-like nature of the Christian is shown in his resemblance to the Lamb of God.'

This ludicrous simile ought to forewarn us that we are in fact reading a shaggy-dog story, a picaresque journey through the realms of higher nonsense. As a student Marx had been infatuated by Laurence Sterne's wildly digressive novel *Tristram Shandy*, and thirty years later he found a subject which allowed him to mimic the loose and disjointed style pioneered by Sterne. Like *Tristram Shandy, Das Kapital* is full of paradoxes and hypotheses, abstruse explanations and whimsical tomfoolery, fractured narratives and curious oddities. How else could he do justice to the mysterious and often topsy-turvy logic of capitalism? As Marx observes, at the end of his exhausting riff about linen and coats: 'A commodity appears at first sight an extremely obvious, trivial thing. But its analysis brings out that it is a very strange thing, abounding in metaphysical subtleties and theological niceties.'

When wood is made into a table, it remains wood for all that – an ordinary, sensuous thing. But when it becomes a commodity it changes into something that transcends sensuousness. 'It not only stands with its feet on the ground, but in relation to all other commodities it stands on its head, and evolves out of its wooden brain grotesque ideas, far more wonderful than if it were to begin dancing of its own free will.' Since different commodities reflect the labour of their producers, the social relationship between human beings 'assumes the fantastic form of a relation between things'. The only analogy Marx can find for this bizarre transformation is in the misty realm of religion: 'There the products of the human brain [i.e. Gods] appear as autonomous figures endowed with a life of their own, which enter into relations both with each other and with the human race. So it is in the world of commodities with the products of men's hands. I call this the fetishism which attaches itself to the products of labour as soon as they are produced as commodities…'

In the religious sense, fetishes are objects venerated for their allegedly supernatural powers, such as the relics of saints in medieval Europe. (As early as 1842, the twenty-four-year-old Marx had ridiculed a German author who claimed that this form of fetishism 'raises man above his sensuous desires' and thus saves him from being a mere animal. Far from raising man above his sensuous desires, Marx riposted, fetishism *is* the religion of sensuous desire: 'Fantasy arising from desire deceives the fetish-worshipper into believing that an inanimate object will give up its natural character in order to comply with his desires.') In a capitalist economy, fetishism is the belief that commodities have some mystical *intrinsic* value. As with the bones of saints, it is a delusion. 'So far,'

Marx writes, 'no chemist has ever discovered exchange-value either in a pearl or a diamond.'

This is a curious example to choose, since it exposes a limitation in Marx's own theory. If, as he implies, the exchange-value of pearls and diamonds derives solely from the labour-time spent on retrieving and transforming them, why do people sometimes pay hundreds of thousands of pounds for a single diamond ring or pearl necklace? Mightn't these extraordinary prices also owe something to scarcity value, or to perceptions of beauty, or even to simple one-upmanship? If labour-time alone were the determinant factor, a doodle on a restaurant napkin by Picasso or a hat once worn by John Lennon would be worth no more than a few pounds – and the 'value' of a bottle of claret from a great vintage would be identical to that of an inferior vintage, if both embody the same quantity of labour.

Marx's more reverential disciples deal with these problems by dismissing them as freakish and irrelevant exceptions to the rule. Besides, didn't Marx himself point out that commodities had 'metaphysical subtleties and theological niceties'? The labour theory of value may be of little assistance in understanding why a few of Elvis Presley's hair-clippings, collected by his barber, sold for $115,000 at auction in 2002; but perhaps the notion of commodity fetishism – 'the magic and necromancy that surrounds the products of labour' – offers at least a partial explanation. In its broadest sense, according to Marx, commodity fetishism represents 'the rule of the object over the human, of dead labour over living, of the product over the producer'. (Here again we see the slow blossoming of an image sown many years earlier. One of his first articles for the *Rheinische Zeitung* in 1842 concerned a new law banning peasants from gathering dead wood in private forests, a right they had enjoyed since medieval times. 'There is the possibility that some young trees may be damaged,' he reported, 'and it needs hardly be said that the wooden idols triumph and human beings are sacrificed!' The idea resurfaced in a speech of 1856 to an audience of Chartists: 'In our days, everything seems pregnant with its contrary... All our invention and progress seem to result in endowing material forces with intellectual life, and in stultifying human life into a material force.') All that is solid melts into air, he wrote in the *Communist Manifesto*; now, in *Das Kapital*, all that is truly human melts into inanimate objects which acquire astounding life and vigour.

Another difficulty then arises, and Marx is willing to tackle this one head-on: *why* are workers tyrannized by and estranged from the objects they create? If value in a commodity is created by labourers, why do they not obtain that full value? In an undeveloped economy, he replies, they often do. 'In that original state of things,' Adam Smith had written in *The Wealth of Nations*, 'which precedes both the appropriation of land and the accumulation of stock, the whole produce of labour belongs to the labourer. He has neither master nor landlord to share with him.' If a carpenter sells a table and uses the money to buy a sack of wheat, the transactions can be described by the formula C–M–C – commodities (C) are transformed into money (M), which is then reconverted into other commodities. But there is another form of commodity circulation, increasingly prevalent under industrial capitalism, which can be written as M–C–M. The capitalist uses money to buy various commodities – labour-power, raw materials, machinery – that produce a new commodity, which is then sold.

Both these circuits can be divided into the same antithetical phases – C–M (sale) and M–C (purchase). What distinguishes them is the order of succession: in one case the starting point and finishing point of the movement are commodities, in the other they are money.

> In the circulation C–M–C, the money is in the end
> converted into a commodity which serves as a use-value; it
> has therefore been spent once and for all. In the inverted
> form M–C–M, on the contrary, the buyer lays out money in
> order that, as a seller, he may recover money… He releases
> the money, but only with the cunning intention of getting it
> back again. The money therefore is not spent, it is merely
> advanced.

Whereas in the 'simple circulation of commodities' represented by C–M–C the twofold displacement of the same piece of money effects its definitive transfer from one hand into another, in M–C–M the twofold displacement of the same commodity causes the money to flow back to its point of departure.

There would be no sense in going through this elaborate rigmarole if the initial investment came back unchanged. So Marx rewrites the formula as M–C–M', where M' is the original sum plus an increment. 'This increment or excess over the original value I call "surplus-value".' And this movement from M to M' is what converts money into capital. Of course, he admits, 'it is also possible that in C–M–C the two extremes C and C, say corn and clothes, may represent quantitatively different magnitudes of value. The peasant may sell his corn above its value, or may buy the clothes at less than their value. He may, on the other hand, be cheated by the clothes merchant.' Yet such differences in value are 'purely accidental' and do not invalidate the essential difference between the two formulae. The simple circulation of commodities – selling in order to buy – is a means to an end, namely the satisfaction of needs. The circulation of money as capital is an end in itself.

It is surplus-value that turns money into capital. But where does surplus-value come from? Marx examines this mystery from the perspective of an apprentice capitalist called Moneybags. Each stage of the circulation – M–C and C–M' – is merely an exchange of equivalents. If goods are exchanged at their real value, it should be impossible for Moneybags to make a profit. More surprisingly, perhaps, the same holds true even if they aren't:

> Suppose... that some inexplicable privilege allows the seller
> to sell his commodities above their value, to sell what is
> worth 100 for 110, therefore with a nominal price increase of

10 per cent. In this case the seller pockets a surplus-value of 10. But after he has sold he becomes a buyer. A third owner of commodities now comes to him as a seller, and he too, for his part, enjoys the privilege of selling his commodities 10 per cent too dear. Our friend [Moneybags] gained 10 as a seller only to lose it again as a buyer. In fact the net result is that all owners of commodities sell their goods to each other at 10 per cent above their value, which is exactly the same as if they sold them at their true value… Everything remains as it was before.

There may be particular instances – as with the peasant and the clothes merchant – where an incorrigibly dim capitalist is hoodwinked into buying commodities at more than their value or selling them too cheaply, but this can hardly be the principle underlying the entire system. To extract surplus-value, our friend Moneybags must find a commodity which has the peculiar property of creating more value in its consumption than it actually cost. Luckily enough, Moneybags discovers a commodity with this unique characteristic – labour-power, which has 'the occult ability to add value to itself. It brings forth living offspring, or at least lays golden eggs.'

Labour-power, according to Marx, is a commodity – in which case its value is measured like that of any other commodity, by the amount of labour-time necessary to produce and reproduce it. (Yet another echo of Adam Smith, who wrote that 'the demand for men necessarily governs the production of men, as of every other commodity'.) It may seem grotesque to assess the worth of human beings as if they were tins of baked beans, but that is precisely Marx's point: for Moneybags, the labour market is no more than another branch of the commodity market. So how does Moneybags assess the value of this particular commodity?

> If the owner of labour-power works today, tomorrow he must again be able to repeat the same process in the same conditions as regards health and strength. His means of subsistence must therefore be sufficient to maintain him in his normal state as a working individual. His natural needs, such as food, clothing, fuel and housing vary according to the climatic and other physical peculiarities of his country. On the other hand, the number and extent of his so-called necessary requirements, as also the manner in which they are satisfied, are themselves products of history… In contrast, therefore, with other commodities, the determination of the value of labour-power contains a historical and moral element. Nevertheless, in a given country at a given period, the average amount of the means of subsistence necessary for the worker is a known *datum*.

Since the worker is mortal, that sum must include 'the means necessary for the worker's replacements, i.e. his children, in order that this race of peculiar commodity owners may perpetuate its presence on the market'. It may also have an element – 'exceedingly small in the case of ordinary labour-power' – for education and training.

Marx calculates that the total required for subsistence is equivalent to about six hours of labour a day. But will Moneybags allow his workers to knock off at the end of their six hours of necessary labour? Certainly not. To earn their wage they must work for another five or six hours, thus providing the 'surplus labour' that creates his profit. 'There is not one single atom of [surplus] value that does not owe its existence to unpaid labour,' Marx concludes, likening this exploitation to 'the age-old activity of the conqueror, who buys commodities from the conquered with the money he has stolen from them'. The only difference from previous epochs is the guile with which the robbery is concealed from the victims.

Having discovered the secret, Moneybags naturally wishes to collect even more eggs from those golden geese. The most obvious method is to make them work longer hours, and in chapter 10 of *Das Kapital*, 'The Working Day', Marx shows the human cost of his impersonal-looking formulae.

The Factory Act of 1850 had limited the British working week to sixty hours. (Sixty hours of actual labour, one should add: with a half-hour for breakfast and an hour for lunch, this meant a twelve-hour shift from Monday to Friday and eight hours on Saturday.) The Act also created a small army of factory inspectors, whose biannual reports armed Marx with detailed proof of 'the voracious appetite of capitalists for surplus labour'. There were countless small thefts from the workers' meal-breaks and recreation times, which added up to a bulging swag-bag: one factory-master boasted to an inspector that shortening meal-breaks by ten minutes a day 'put one thousand a year in my pocket'. The bourgeois press provided further ammunition. A *Daily Telegraph* report on the lace trade in Nottingham revealed that 'children of nine or ten years are dragged from their squalid beds at two, three, or four o'clock in the morning and compelled to work for a bare subsistence until ten, eleven or twelve at night, their limbs wearing away, their frames dwindling, their faces whitening, and their humanity absolutely sinking into a stone-like torpor, utterly horrible to contemplate'.

There is a strong echo here of Friedrich Engels's *Condition of the Working Class in England* (1845), which interwove personal observations with damning information from newspapers, parliamentary commissions, factory inspectors and copies of Hansard. 'I delight in the testimony of my opponents,' Engels had written, happily amazed that the British establishment had published so much evidence against itself. The citations from government 'blue books' and *Economist* articles in *Das Kapital* show how much Karl Marx learned from this technique.

The chapter on the working day, one of the longest in the book, is a compendium of horror stories, framed by Marx in suitably Gothic style. 'Capital is dead labour which, vampire-like, lives only by sucking living labour, and lives the more, the more labour it sucks,' he writes in his introductory paragraphs. More than seventy pages later, after a banquet of gore, he concludes that 'the vampire will not let go'. To protect themselves from this bloodsucker, the workers 'have to put their heads together and, as a class, compel the passing of a law, an all-powerful social barrier by which they can be prevented from selling themselves and their families into slavery and death by voluntary contract with capital'. But he admits that such a law would not in itself be enough to thwart Moneybags and his fellow capitalists, for they have another way of increasing productivity and therefore surplus-value.

If labour-power really is a uniquely valuable commodity, one might expect competition among employers to drive wages up – and in times of full employment this may indeed be the case. As the cost of labour rises, however, Moneybags finds that investment in labour-saving machinery, which might once have seemed uneconomic, now makes financial sense, especially if he cannot lengthen the working day. As Marx writes, 'Capital... has an immanent drive, and a constant tendency, towards increasing the productivity of labour, in order to cheapen commodities and, by cheapening commodities, to cheapen the worker himself.'

In theory, machines could ease the burden of the labourer. Under a system of capitalist production, Marx argues, their effects are invariably malign – though highly beneficial to Mr Moneybags. (His chapter on industrial machinery begins with a quote from John Stuart Mill's *Principles of Political Economy*: 'It is questionable if all the mechanical inventions yet made have lightened the day's toil of any human being.') By substituting its own awesome productive ability for independent human strength the machine leaves the worker increasingly subordinate to capital. He is deskilled precisely because of the inhuman skill of the automatons, and his ability to defend his position through combining with other workers – through craft associations, for instance – diminishes while the machines themselves combine into an ever more potent force. It is, as so often in *Das Kapital,* a vision from a horror story: 'Here we have, in place of the isolated machine, a mechanical monster whose body fills whole factories, and whose demonic power, at first hidden by the slow and measured motions of its gigantic members, finally bursts forth in the fast and feverish whirl of its countless working organs.' In so far as machinery dispenses with the need for human brawn it also becomes a means of employing children, who have slighter physiques but more supple limbs, and thus it revolutionizes the contract between worker and capitalist:

> Taking the exchange of commodities as our basis, our
> first assumption was that the capitalist and the worker
> confronted each other as free persons, the independent
> owners, the one possessing money and the means of
> production, the other labour-power. But now the capitalist
> buys children and young persons…

Marx notes that advertisements for child labourers often resemble the inquiries for Negro slaves which formerly appeared in American newspapers, citing one reported by a British factory inspector: 'Wanted, 12 to 20 young persons, not younger than what can pass for 13 years. Wages 4 shillings a week.' The significance of the phrase 'what can pass for 13 years' was that under the Factory Act children below that age could work only six hours a day. An officially appointed doctor had to certify their age, and Marx observes that the apparent decline in the number of children under thirteen working in industry during the 1850s and 1860s 'was for the most part, according to the evidence of the factory inspectors themselves, the work of the certifying surgeons, who adjusted the children's ages in a manner appropriate to the capitalist's greed for exploitation and the parents' need to engage in this traffic'.

The capitalist application of technology produces a form of perpetual motion. A machine working sixteen hours a day for seven and a half years produces as much as the same machine working only eight hours a day for fifteen years. Although it transmits to the finished product no more surplus-value, it allows the capitalist to absorb that profit twice as quickly. So there is a strong incentive to use the machinery for as many hours per day as possible by lengthening the machine-minders' shifts – and they are in no position to resist, since automation has also intensified the competition for jobs by creating what Marx calls an 'industrial reserve army' of the unemployed. This surplus population of workers is not only a necessary by-product of industrial capitalism; it also becomes, conversely, a *lever* of capitalist accumulation by providing 'a mass of human material always ready for exploitation'. When a market expands quickly or opens new branches, as with the railways, 'there must be the possibility of suddenly throwing great masses of men into the decisive areas without doing any damage to the scale of production in other spheres. The surplus population supplies these masses.' The cyclic pattern of modern industry – a period of average activity, followed by production at high pressure, crisis and stagnation – depends on the constant formation, absorption and re-formation of the industrial reserve army. The various phases of this cycle recruit the surplus population but also become energetic agencies for its reproduction.

Surplus labour in turn regulates the general movements of wages. As Marx writes:

> The industrial reserve army, during the periods of stagnation and average prosperity, weighs down the active army of workers; during the periods of over-production and feverish activity, it puts a curb on their pretensions. The relative surplus population is therefore the background against which the law of the demand and supply of labour does its work.

Marx has no illusions about the supposedly sacred symmetry of the law of supply and demand. The demand for labour is not identical with an increase in the supply of capital, since 'it is not a case of two independent forces working on each other. The dice are loaded.' Here he takes a swipe at 'one of the great exploits of economic apologetics' – the notion peddled by several mid-Victorian economists that the introduction of new machinery, or the extension of old, somehow 'sets free' the workers. They are set free, he maintains, only in the sense that they are out of a job altogether, 'and every new bit of capital looking round for a function can take advantage of them'. When they do find employment, fear of rejoining the reserve army leaves them riper for exploitation. So, he concludes, the greater the productivity of labour, the greater the 'relative mass' of the industrial reserve army. The consequence of a rise in social wealth is therefore an increase in official pauperism. *'This is the absolute general law of capitalist accumulation,'* he declares, in a fine italicized fanfare – then bathetically undermines this in the very next sentence: 'Like all other laws, it is modified in its working by many circumstances, the analysis of which does not concern us here.'

Having sidestepped any objections, Marx proceeds to one of the most notorious assertions in *Das Kapital:* that capitalism leads to the progressive 'immiseration' or impoverishment of the proletariat. Countless pundits have taken this to mean that capitalism's swelling prosperity would be achieved by an absolute reduction in the workers' wages and standard of living, and they have found it easy to mock. Look at the working classes of today, with their cars and microwave ovens: not very immiserated, are they? The American economist Paul Samuelson has said that Marx's entire *œuvre* can safely be disregarded because the impoverishment of the workers 'simply never took place' – and, since Samuelson's textbooks have been the staple fare for generations of undergraduates in both Britain and America, this has become the received wisdom.

But it is a myth, based on a misreading of 'The General Law of Capitalist Accumulation' in chapter 25 of the first volume. 'Pauperism,' Marx writes, 'forms a condition of capitalist production, and of the capitalist development of wealth. It forms part of the incidental expenses of capitalist production: but capital usually knows how to transfer those from its own shoulders to those of the working class and the petty bourgeoisie.' In the context, he is clearly referring not to the whole proletariat but to the 'lowest sediment' of society, such as the permanently unemployed, the sick, the ragged – a stratum which still exists today, and is now often called the underclass. (Another Jewish outcast said that 'the poor ye have always with you', but no economist has yet suggested that Jesus's teachings are wholly discredited by his prediction of eternal immiseration. Even Leszek Kolakowski, one of Marx's most influential twentieth-century critics, has conceded that 'material pauperization was not a necessary premiss either of Marx's analysis of the dehumanization caused by wage labour or of his prediction of the inescapable ruin of capitalism'.)

What Marx did say was that under capitalism there would be a *relative* – not absolute – decline in wages. This is demonstrably true: no firm enjoying a 20 per cent increase in surplus-value will hand over all the loot to its workforce in the form of a 20 per cent pay rise. 'It follows therefore,' Marx writes, 'that in proportion as capital accumulates, the situation of the worker, be his payment high or low, must grow worse.' The crucial phrase here is 'be his payment high or low': labour lags further and further behind capital, no matter how many cars and microwave ovens the workers can afford.

Besides, Marx makes it abundantly clear in the very same paragraph that his definition of poverty (like Christ's) goes far beyond pounds and pence: it is about the crushing of the human spirit. With the worker chained to capital 'more firmly than the wedges of Hephaestus held Prometheus to the rock', misery for some becomes a necessary condition for the wealth of others:

> Within the capitalist system all methods for raising the social productivity of labour are put into effect at the cost of the individual worker... they distort the worker into a fragment of a man, they degrade him to the level of an appendage of a machine, they destroy the actual content of his labour by turning it into a torment; they alienate him from the intellectual potentialities of the labour process in the same proportion as science is incorporated in it as an independent power; they deform the conditions under which he works, subject him during the labour process to a despotism the more hateful for its meanness; they transform his lifetime into working-time, and drag his wife and child beneath the wheels of the juggernaut of capital... Accumulation of wealth at one pole is, therefore, at the same time accumulation of misery, the torment of labour, slavery, ignorance, brutalization and moral degradation at the opposite pole, i.e. on the side of the class that produces its own product as capital.

That last sentence, taken alone, could be adduced as another prediction of absolute financial impoverishment for the workers, but only a halfwit – or an economics lecturer – could hold to this interpretation after reading the thunderous philippic which precedes it.

In the 1970s there was much talk of an imminent 'leisure age' in which, thanks to automation, we would scarcely work at all – and a spate of books brooding earnestly on how we would fill our new spare time without becoming hopelessly lethargic. Anybody spotting one of these forgotten tracts in a second-hand bookshop today would laugh incredulously. The average British employee now puts in 80,224 hours over his or her working life, as against 69,000 hours in 1981. Far from losing the work ethic, we seem ever more enslaved by it. The new vogue is for books that ask anxiously how we can achieve a 'work–life balance' in an age when many people have no time for anything beyond labour and sleep.

This would not have surprised Karl Marx. In chapter 12 of *Das Kapital* he debunks those mid-Victorian economic treatises in which 'we may read on one page that the worker owes a debt of gratitude to capital for developing his productivity, because the necessary labour-time is thereby shortened, and on the next page that he must prove his gratitude by working in future for 15 hours instead of 10'. What capitalist production aims at, he says, is not a reduction of the working day but a minimizing of the labour-time necessary for producing a commodity. 'The fact that the worker, when the productivity of his labour has been increased, produces ten times as many commodities as before, and thus spends one-tenth as much labour-time on each, by no means prevents him from continuing to work 12 hours as before, nor from producing in those 12 hours 1,200 articles instead of 120. Indeed, his working day may simultaneously be prolonged, so as to make him produce 1,400 articles in 14 hours.' The objective of this process is 'the shortening of that part of the working day in which the worker must work for himself and the lengthening, thereby, of the other part of the day, in which he is free to work for nothing for the capitalist'.

But if all these extra commodities flood into the market while the workers (in their role as consumers) are no richer than before, the capitalist will be left with a huge pile of unsold products. What then? In the *Communist Manifesto* of 1848 Marx had already drawn attention to 'the commercial crises that by their periodical return put on trial, each time more threateningly, the existence of the entire bourgeois society. In these crises a great part not only of the existing products, but also of the previously created productive forces, are periodically destroyed. In these crises there breaks out an epidemic that, in all earlier epochs, would have seemed an absurdity – the epidemic of over-production.' The conditions of bourgeois society, he argued, were simply too narrow to comprise the wealth created by them. Capitalism had two ways of surmounting the problem: 'On the one hand by enforced destruction of a mass of productive forces; on the other, by the conquest of new markets, and by the more thorough exploitation of the old ones. That is to say, by paving the way for more extensive and more destructive crises, and by diminishing the means whereby crises are prevented.'

This is the cycle of 'boom and bust' from which governments have struggled to escape ever since. According to Marx no escape was possible so long as capitalism prevailed: the tidal rhythm of expansion and recession was integral to a system with a natural tendency towards over-production. 'The real barrier of capitalist production,' he wrote in Volume III of *Das Kapital*, 'is capital itself.' If the preservation of capital's value rests on expropriating and pauperizing the mass of people, it will always come into conflict with capital's simultaneous drive towards an unlimited and unconditional extension of productivity. 'The last cause of all real crises always remains the poverty and restricted consumption of the masses as compared to the tendency of capitalist production to develop the productive forces in such a way that only the absolute power of consumption of the entire society would be their limit.'

Capitalism was thus threatened with mortal injury by its own weapons. After the failure of the 1848 uprisings Marx had argued that a new revolution was possible 'only in consequence of a new [economic] crisis', and he had been waiting impatiently ever since for the cataclysm to arrive. At Christmas 1851 he predicted that it 'must blow up at the latest next autumn… I am more than ever convinced that there will be no serious revolution without a trade crisis.' Every flutter in the markets or rash of bankruptcies brought similar gleeful forecasts. 'On top of that there is the commercial crisis which is looming ever closer and whose early symptoms are erupting on every hand. *Les choses marchent'* (1852). 'Present conditions… in my view must soon lead to an earthquake' (1853). His expectations were continually reinforced by Friedrich Engels, his agent in the citadel of capitalism, who informed him in 1856 that within the next year there would be 'a day of wrath such as has never been seen before; the whole of Europe's industry in ruins, all markets over-stocked… all the propertied classes in the soup, complete bankruptcy of the bourgeoisie, war and profligacy to the nth degree.' In the winter of 1857–8, as we have seen, Marx worked furiously on the economic notebooks which became the *Grundrisse* 'so that at least I get the outlines clear before the *déluge*'. He returned to the theme in an afterword to the second edition of Volume I of *Das Kapital* (1873), written to defend its dialectical style:

> In its rational form [the dialectic] is a scandal and an abomination to the bourgeoisie and its doctrinaire spokesmen, because it includes in its positive understanding of what exists a simultaneous recognition of its negation, its inevitable destruction… The fact that the movement of capitalist society is full of contradictions impresses itself most strikingly on the practical bourgeois in the changes of the periodic cycle through which modern industry passes, the summit of which is the general crisis. That crisis is once again approaching…

When it arrived, he added, its intensity and universality would 'drum dialectics even into the heads of the upstarts in charge of the new Holy Prussian-German Empire'.

A vain hope: almost a century and a half later, Marx's use of the dialectic in *Das Kapital* remains a matter of hot dispute. The method derives from his early study of Hegel, who synthesized many previous dialectical forms – from Zeno's paradoxes to Kantian critique – into what can best be summarized as a self-generating process of reason. Hegel himself called it 'the grasping of opposites in their unity or of the positive in the negative', the pursuit of contradictions and their incorporation into new and fuller ideas. Every idea is the product of a less developed phase of that idea, but contains within it the germ of a more advanced notion.

The relevance of this to Marx's own conception of economic progress is clear enough – though Hegel, being an idealist rather than a materialist, would undoubtedly have protested at the inversion of his technique. For Hegel, the real world is nothing but an expression of 'the Idea', whereas for Marx the Idea is nothing but the material world reflected in the human mind and translated into forms of thought. 'Hegel's dialectics is the basic form of all dialectics,' Marx writes, 'but only *after* it has been stripped of its mystified form, and it is precisely this which distinguishes my method.' In that 1873 afterword he recalls that he criticized the mystificatory side of Hegel's dialectic almost thirty years earlier, at a time when it was still the fashion.

> But just when I was working at the first volume of *Das Kapital*, the ill-humoured, arrogant and mediocre epigones

who now talk large in educated German circles began to take pleasure in treating Hegel… as a 'dead dog'. I therefore openly avowed myself the pupil of that mighty thinker, and even, here and there in the chapter on the theory of value, coquetted with the mode of expression peculiar to him.

As Marx knew, however, these dialectical dalliances had an extra use-value. After writing an article on the Indian mutiny in 1857, suggesting that the British would begin their retreat as soon as the rainy season started, he had confessed to Engels: 'It's possible that I shall make an ass of myself. But in that case one can always get out of it with a little dialectic. I have, of course, so worded my proposition as to be right either way.' When applied like this, dialectic means never having to admit that one was wrong.

Even the most apparently unambiguous prophecy in *Das Kapital* – the imminent demise of capitalism – can thus elude the critical blow-torch of those who seek to falsify it. In the peroration to Volume I, Marx asserts that competition between capitalists concentrates production into ever larger units, which intensify the oppression and exploitation of labour, 'but with this too grows the revolt of the working class, a class always increasing in numbers, and disciplined, united, organized by the very mechanism of the process of capitalist production itself… The knell of capitalist private property sounds.' Most readers deduce from this that Marx thought capitalism was already on its death-bed – a reasonable inference, given the apocalyptic glee with which he greeted each new financial crisis. ('Present conditions… in my view must soon lead to an earthquake.') Yet it would be a surprising assumption for Marx, of all people, to make. His own account of the various historical phases of economic production – primitive-communal, ancient, feudal, capitalist – notes that each era lasted for many centuries, sometimes even millennia, before yielding to its successor. And Marx recognizes that bourgeois capitalism is far more dynamic and powerful than any earlier mode: as he wrote in the *Communist Manifesto,* 'it has accomplished wonders far surpassing Egyptian pyramids, Roman aqueducts and Gothic cathedrals; it has conducted expeditions that put in the shade all former Exoduses of nations and crusades.' How, then, could he have believed that this awesome force would fizzle out after only a century or two?

Perhaps he didn't. Volume I may have sounded capitalism's death-knell, but in the final chapter of Volume II a 'schematic presentation' of hypothetical calculations provides an economic model of a capitalist economy which grows steadily without recurrent crises and could in theory continue indefinitely. Although Marx yearns for the collapse of capitalism and an end to exploitation – a yearning that occasionally erupts in blood-curdling prophecies of doom – the force of his rhetoric is qualified and nuanced when one studies his work as a whole. Marx has often been portrayed as a mechanical determinist who saw the world in terms of iron laws and inevitable consequences, but it is a caricature. True, he claimed in the *Communist Manifesto* that the fall of the bourgeoisie and the victory of the proletariat 'are equally inevitable'; in *The*

Eighteenth Brumaire of Louis Bonaparte (1852), however, he added that 'men make their own history, but they do not make it just as they please; they do not make it under circumstances chosen by themselves, but under circumstances directly encountered, given and transmitted from the past.'

The original preface to *Das Kapital* promises to outline the 'natural laws of capitalist production... working themselves out with iron necessity'. Yet as a former legal student himself, Marx knows that the mere existence of a law against, say, theft does not mean that all thieving ceases. This is particularly apparent with one of his most controversial formulations, the so-called law of the falling rate of profit.

The idea that the rate of profit would decline as an economy developed was common to all classical economists, including Adam Smith and David Ricardo, though they disagreed on *why* this should happen. Smith attributed it to a waning of profitable opportunities; Ricardo thought that a finite supply of land would cause rents to rise, thus reducing profit margins. Marx's version, outlined in Volume III, is that competition among manufacturers will oblige them to invest more in 'constant capital' (plant and machinery) and therefore proportionately less in 'variable capital' (wages). If, as he believed, human labour is the source of exchange-value, then the rate of profit – if not its actual total – must fall. 'It is thereby proved a logical necessity that in its development the general average rate of surplus-value must express itself in a falling general rate of profit.'

There have been many attacks on this bold, undersubstantiated assertion, and Marx seems to have expected them. In the very next chapter he tries to find reasons why in practice the rate of profit has not fallen as his theory would require. One is foreign trade: cheaply produced imports allow for a higher profit margin. There is also the familiar point about the industrial reserve army: increased productivity makes workers redundant and forces down wages, so slowing the tendency to replace human labour with expensive machinery. In short, there are 'counteracting influences at work, which cross and annul the effect of the general law, and which give it merely the characteristic of a tendency'. Indeed, 'the same influences which produce a tendency in the general rate of profit to fall also call forth counter-effects, which hamper, retard and partly paralyse this fall'. Once again, it looks as if he is rewording his proposition so as to be right either way.

Similar qualifications can be found in his discussion of those endemic crises of over-production (or, looked at from the other side, under-consumption). The first consequence of a recession, when it arrives, is a huge fall in prices and depreciation of capital. But this restores the rate of profit, enabling investment and growth to resume. Or, as Marx puts it in Volume III of *Das Kapital*: 'The stagnation in production that has intervened prepares the ground for a later expansion of production – within the capitalist limits. And so we go round the whole circle. One part of the capital that was devalued by the cessation of its function regains its old value. And apart from that, with expanded conditions of production, a wider market and increased productivity, the same cycle of errors is pursued once more.' Couldn't one therefore regard these periodic tremors as nothing more than a self-correcting mechanism, ensuring the perpetual survival of the system rather than precipitating its downfall? In the words of Leon Trotsky, 'capitalism does live by crises and booms, just as a human being lives by inhaling and exhaling'.

Nowhere in *Das Kapital* does Marx explain why or how – still less when – the system will ultimately destroy itself. He simply states it as his conviction: each new slump leads to a greater concentration of capital, and this monopoly becomes a fetter on the mode of production until 'centralization of the means of production and socialization of labour at last reach a point where they become incompatible with their capitalist integument. This integument is burst asunder... The expropriators are expropriated.' With this happy prospect he ends the first (and only complete) volume of *Das Kapital*.

Well, almost. After his resounding peroration, Marx decided to add an ironic coda in the form of a chapter on 'the modern theory of colonization', designed to show what happens if wage-labourers can break free of their shackles. In countries such as England, the capitalist regime has so thoroughly subordinated to itself the nation's resources that economists see it as part of the natural order. But Marx notices that 'it is otherwise in the colonies', where Mr Moneybags comes up against the obstacle of working-class settlers who use their labour to enrich themselves instead of the capitalist. ('It's a splendid thing,' Engels had written to Marx in September 1851, following the discovery of gold in southern

Australia. 'The British will be thrown out and the united states of deported murderers, burglars, rapists and pickpockets will startle the world by demonstrating what wonders can be performed by a state consisting of undisguised rascals.')

The defining anecdote in this final chapter is the tragicomic tale of a Mr Peel, who took with him from England to the Swan River district of western Australia £50,000 in cash and 3,000 working-class men, women and children. He overlooked only one thing: the need to keep his workers separated from the means of production. Finding land freely available in this empty region they abandoned their employer, leaving him without even a servant to make his bed or fetch him water from the river. 'Unhappy Mr Peel,' Marx writes, 'who provided for everything except the export of English relations of production to the Swan River!'

Marx found the Peel story in a book by the businessman Edward Gibbon Wakefield, who cited it as an example of the dire consequences of spontaneous and unregulated colonization. At the Swan River Settlement, Wakefield complained, 'a great mass of capital, of seeds, implements and cattle, has perished for want of labourers to use it, and... no settler has preserved much more capital than he can employ with his own hands'. In the northern states of America, too, 'it may be doubted whether so many as a tenth of the people would fall under the description of hired labourers'. When given the chance, workers ceased to be labour-for-hire and became independent producers – perhaps even 'competitors with their former masters in the labour market'. To remedy this shocking state of affairs, Wakefield advocated 'systematic colonization', which would ensure a supply of subservient and dependent labourers, not all that different in function and status from slaves. It could easily be achieved by setting an artificially high price on the virgin soil, placing it beyond the reach of ordinary wage-earners and so compelling them to work for poor Mr Peel.

One can see why Marx takes such pleasure in this frank admission of capitalism's requirements. 'It is the great merit of E. G. Wakefield,' he writes, 'to have discovered, not something new *about* the colonies, but, in the colonies, the truth about capitalist relations in the mother country… that the capitalist mode of production and accumulation, and therefore capitalist private property as well, have for their fundamental condition the annihilation of that private property which rests on the labour of the individual himself; in other words, the expropriation of the worker.' The fact that Marx chose this as the final sentence of the book tells us much about his authorial intentions. Had he ended with integuments bursting asunder and expropriators being expropriated, *Das Kapital* might be taken as essentially a prophetic work about the inevitable doom of capitalism. Instead, he turns again to the victims rather than the oppressors, leaving us with a restatement of the dominant *motif*: whatever its fate, whether it lasts for a century or a millennium, capitalism depends on exploitation.

We are back where we began, in an earthly hell that resembles a secular version of Dante's *Inferno*. 'What does it matter to you what people whisper here?' Virgil asks Dante in Canto

5 of the *Purgatorio*. 'Follow me and let the people talk. *[Vien retro a me, e lascia dir le genti.]*' Lacking a Virgil to guide him, Marx amends the line in his preface for the first volume of *Das Kapital* to warn that he will make no concession to the prejudices of others: 'Now, as ever, my maxim is that of the great Florentine: *Segui il tuo corso, e lascia dir le genti.* [Go your own way, and let the people talk.]' From the outset, then, the book is conceived as a descent towards the nether regions, and even in the midst of complex theoretical abstractions he conveys a vivid sense of place and motion:

> Let us, therefore, leave this noisy region of the market, where all that goes on is done in full view of everyone's eyes, where everything seems open and above board. We will follow the owner of the money and the owner of labour-power into the hidden foci of production, crossing the threshold of the portal above which is written, 'No admittance except on business'. Here we shall discover, not only how capital produces, but also how it is itself produced. We shall at last discover the secret of making surplus value.

The literary antecedents for such a journey are often recalled as he proceeds on his way. Describing English match-factories, where half the workers are juveniles (some as young as six) and conditions are so appalling that 'only the most miserable part of the working class, half-starved widows and so forth, deliver up their children to it', he writes:

> With a working day ranging from 12 to 14 or 15 hours, night-labour, irregular meal-times, and meals mostly taken in the workrooms themselves, pestilent with phosphorus, Dante would have found the worst horrors in his *Inferno* surpassed in this industry.

Other imagined hells provide further embellishment for his picture of empirical reality:

> From the motley crowd of workers of all callings, ages and sexes, who throng around us more urgently than did the souls of the slain around Ulysses, on whom we see at a glance the signs of overwork, without referring to the Blue Books under their arms, let us select two more figures, whose striking contrast proves that all men are alike in the face of capital – a milliner and a blacksmith.

This is the cue for a story about Mary Anne Walkley, a twenty-year-old girl who died 'from simple overwork' after labouring uninterruptedly for more than twenty-six hours making millinery for the guests at a ball given by the Princess of Wales in 1863. Her employer ('a lady with the pleasant name of Elise', as Marx notes caustically) was dismayed to find that the girl had died without finishing the bit of finery she was stitching.

If these characters hadn't existed, Charles Dickens might have been obliged to invent them. There is a Dickensian texture to much of *Das Kapital*, and Marx gives the occasional explicit nod to an author whom he loved. Here, for example, is how he swats bourgeois apologists who claim that his criticisms of particular applications of technology reveal him as an enemy of social progress who doesn't want machinery to be used at all:

> This is exactly the reasoning of Bill Sikes, the celebrated cut-throat. 'Gentlemen of the jury, no doubt the throat of this commercial traveller has been cut. But that is not my fault, it is the fault of the knife. Must we, for such a temporary inconvenience, abolish the use of the knife? Only consider! Where would agriculture and trade be without the knife? Is it not as salutary in surgery as it is skilled in anatomy? And a willing assistant at the festive table? If you abolish the knife – you hurl us back into the depths of barbarism.'

Bill Sikes makes no such speech in *Oliver Twist*: this is Marx's satirical extrapolation. 'They are my slaves,' he would sometimes say, gesturing at the books on his shelves, 'and they must serve me as I will.' The task of this unpaid workforce was to provide raw materials which could then be shaped for his own purposes. 'His conversation does not run in one groove, but is as varied as are the volumes upon his library shelves,' wrote an interviewer from the *Chicago Tribune* who visited Marx in 1878. 'A man can generally be judged by the books he reads, and you can form your own conclusions when I tell you a casual glance revealed Shakespeare, Dickens, Thackeray, Molière, Racine, Montaigne, Bacon, Goethe, Voltaire, Paine; English, American, French blue books; works political and philosophical in Russian, German, Spanish, Italian, etc, etc.' Et cetera indeed: in 1976 Professor S. S. Prawer wrote a 450-page book devoted entirely to Marx's literary references. The first volume of *Das Kapital* yielded quotations from the Bible, Shakespeare, Goethe, Milton, Voltaire, Homer, Balzac, Dante, Schiller, Sophocles, Plato, Thucydides, Xenophon, Defoe, Cervantes, Dryden, Heine, Virgil, Juvenal, Horace, Thomas More, Samuel Butler – as well as allusions to horror tales about werewolves and vampires, German chap-books, English romantic novels, popular ballads, songs and jingles, melodrama and farce, myths and proverbs.

What of *Das Kapital*'s own literary status? Marx knew that it could not be won second-hand, by the mere display of other men's flowers. In Volume I he scorns those economists who 'conceal under a parade of literary-historical erudition, or by an admixture of extraneous material, their feeling of scientific impotence and the eerie consciousness of having to teach others what they themselves felt to be a truly strange subject'. A fear that he could himself have committed this offence may explain the anguished admission, in the afterword to its second edition, that 'no one can feel the literary shortcomings of *Das Kapital* more strongly than I'. Even so, it is surprising that so few people have even considered the book as literature. *Das Kapital* has spawned countless texts analysing Marx's labour theory of value or his law of the declining rate of profit, but only a handful of critics have given serious attention to Marx's own declared ambition – in several letters to Engels – to produce a work of art.

One deterrent, perhaps, is that the multilayered structure of *Das Kapital* evades easy categorization. The book can be read as a vast Gothic novel whose heroes are enslaved and consumed by the monster they created ('Capital which comes into the world soiled with gore from top to toe and oozing blood from every pore'); or as a Victorian melodrama (in his 1962 study, *The Tangled Bank: Darwin, Marx, Frazer and Freud as Imaginative Writers*, S. E. Hyman even proposes an apt title for the drama: 'The Mortgage on Labour-Power Foreclosed'); or as a black farce (in debunking the 'phantom-like objectivity' of the commodity to expose the difference between heroic appearance and inglorious reality Marx is using one of the classic methods of comedy, stripping off the gallant knight's armour to reveal a tubby little man in his underpants); or as a Greek tragedy ('Like Oedipus, the actors in Marx's recounting of human history are in the grip of an inexorable necessity which unfolds itself no matter what they do,' C. Frankel writes in *Marx and Contemporary Scientific Thought*. 'And yet all that links them to this fate is their own tragic blindness, their own *idées fixes*, which prevent them from seeing the facts until too late'). Or perhaps it is a satirical utopia like the land of the Houyhnhnms in *Gulliver's Travels*, where every prospect pleases and only man is vile: in Marx's version of capitalist society, as in Jonathan Swift's equine pseudo-paradise, the false Eden is created by reducing ordinary humans to the status of impotent, alienated Yahoos.

To do justice to the deranged logic of capitalism, Marx's text is saturated with irony – an irony which has yet escaped most scholars for the past 140 years. One exception is the American critic Edmund Wilson, who argued in *To The Finland Station: a study in the writing and acting of history* (1940) that the value of Marx's abstractions – the dance of commodities, the zany cross-stitch of value – is primarily an ironic one, juxtaposed as they are with grim, well-documented scenes of the misery and filth which capitalist laws create in practice. Wilson regarded *Das Kapital* as a parody of classical economics, 'and once we have read [it] the conventional works on economics never seem the same to us again: we can always see through their arguments and figures the realities of the crude human relations which it is their purpose or effect to mask'. No one, he thought, had ever had so deadly a psychological insight into the infinite capacity of human nature for remaining oblivious or indifferent to the pains we inflict on others when we have a chance to get something out of them for ourselves. 'In dealing with this theme, Karl Marx became one of the great masters of satire. Marx is certainly the greatest ironist since Swift, and has a good deal in common with him.'

This tribute seems so hyperbolic or downright incredible that supporting evidence may be required. So let us turn to the posthumous *Theories of Surplus-Value,* the so-called fourth volume of *Das Kapital,* in which Marx recounts the various attempts by classical economists to distinguish between 'productive' and 'unproductive' labour. In the latter class Adam Smith had placed 'churchmen, lawyers, physicians, men of letters of all kinds; players, buffoons, musicians, opera-singers, opera-dancers, etc', all of whom 'are maintained by a part of the annual produce of the *industry of other people'*. But is the distinction really so clear and simple? Marx suggests that every conceivable occupation *can* be productive, and sets out to prove it with an apparently absurd example:

> A philosopher produces ideas, a poet poems, a clergyman sermons, a professor books and so on. A criminal produces crimes. If we look a little closer at the connection between this latter branch of production and society as a whole, we shall rid ourselves of many prejudices. The criminal produces not only crimes but also criminal law, and with this also the professor who gives lectures on criminal law and in addition to this the inevitable book in which this same professor throws his lectures onto the general market as 'commodities'…

The criminal moreover produces the whole of the police and of criminal justice, constables, judges, hangmen, juries, etc; and all these different lines of business, which form equally many categories of the social division of labour, develop different capacities of the human spirit, create new needs and new ways of satisfying them. Torture alone has given rise to the most ingenious mechanical inventions, and employed many honourable craftsmen in the production of its instruments.

The criminal produces an impression, partly moral and partly tragic, as the case may be, and in this way renders a 'service' by arousing the moral and aesthetic feelings of the public. He produces not only books on criminal law, not only penal codes and along with them legislators in this field, but also art, belles-lettres, novels, and even tragedies, as not only Müllner's *Schuld* and Schiller's *Räuber* show, but also *Oedipus* and *Richard the Third.* [If he were writing today, he could add that without crime there'd be no John Grisham, no Inspector Morse, no Tony Soprano, nor even James Bond.] The criminal breaks the monotony and everyday security of bourgeois life. In this way he keeps it from stagnation, and gives rise to that uneasy tension and agility without which even the spur of competition would get blunted...

> The effects of the criminal on the development of productive power can be shown in detail. Would locks ever have reached their present degree of excellence had there been no thieves? Would the making of banknotes have reached its present perfection had there been no forgers?... And if one leaves the sphere of private crime: would the world-market ever have come into being but for national crime? Indeed, would even the nations have arisen? And hasn't the Tree of Sin been at the same time the Tree of Knowledge ever since the time of Adam?

As Edmund Wilson says, this stands comparison with Swift's modest proposal for curing the misery of Ireland by persuading the starving poor to eat their surplus babies.

Ultimately, however, even Wilson loses the plot. Only a

few pages after praising Marx's keen psychological insight and elevating him to the pantheon of satirical genius, he protests at 'the crudity of the psychological motivation which underlies the world view of Marx' and complains that the theory propounded in *Das Kapital* is 'simply, like the dialectic, a creation of the metaphysician who never abdicated before the economist in Marx'. This sounds very like those German reviews of the first volume which accused Marx of 'Hegelian sophistry' – a charge to which he was happy to plead guilty, admitting that in *Das Kapital* he coquetted with Hegel's mode of expression. The dialectical flirtations which so offend Edmund Wilson are all of a piece with the irony he admires so highly: both techniques up-end apparent reality to disclose its guilty secrets. As the American philosopher Robert Paul Wolff commented in a 1984 lecture, 'it is an odd sort of compliment to call a writer the greatest ironist since Swift, and then to adjudge his most serious intellectual efforts crackpot metaphysics'.

What, then, is the connection between Marx's ironic literary discourse and his 'metaphysical' account of bourgeois society? Or, as Wolff puts the question: 'Why *must* Marx write as he does if he is to accomplish the intellectual tasks he has set for himself?' Had he wished to produce a straightforward text of classical economics he could have done so – and in fact he did. Two lectures delivered in June 1865, later published as *Value, Price and Profit,* give a concise and lucid précis of his theories about commodities and labour: 'A man who produces an article for his own immediate use, to consume it himself, creates a *product* but not a *commodity*... A commodity has a *value,* because it is a *crystallization of social labour... Price,* taken by itself, is nothing but the *monetary expression of value...* What the working man sells is not directly his *labour,* but his *labouring power,* the temporary disposal of which he makes over to the capitalist...' And so on. Whatever its merits as an economic analysis, this can be understood by any intelligent child: no elaborate metaphors or metaphysics, no puzzling digressions or philosophical excursions, no literary flourishes. So why is *Das Kapital,* which covers the same ground, so utterly different in style? Did Marx suddenly lose the gift of plain speaking? Manifestly not: at the time he gave these lectures he was also completing the first volume of *Das Kapital.* A clue can be found in one of the very few analogies he permitted himself in *Value, Price and Profit,* when explaining his belief that profits arise from selling commodities at their 'real' value and not, as one might suppose, from adding a surcharge. 'This seems paradox and contrary to everyday observation,' he writes. 'It is also paradox that the earth moves round the sun, and that water consists of two highly inflammable gases. Scientific truth is always paradox, if judged by everyday experience, which catches only the delusive nature of things.'

The function of metaphor is to make us look at something anew by transferring its qualities to something else, turning the familiar into the alien or vice versa. Ludovico Silva, a Mexican critic of Marx, has drawn on the etymological meaning of 'metaphor' as a transfer to argue that capitalism itself is a metaphor, an alienating process which displaces life from subject to object, from use-value to exchange-value, from the human to the monstrous. In this reading, the literary style Marx adopted in *Das Kapital* is not a colourful veneer applied to an otherwise forbidding slab of economic exposition, like jam on thick toast; it is the only appropriate language in which to express 'the delusive nature of things', an ontological enterprise which cannot be confined within the borders and conventions of an existing genre such as political economy, anthropological science or history. In short, *Das Kapital* is entirely *sui generis.* There has been nothing remotely like it before or since – which is probably why it has been so consistently neglected or misconstrued.

CHAPTER 3

Afterlife

A century after its publication, the British prime minister Harold Wilson boasted that he had never read *Das Kapital*. 'I only got as far as page two – that's where the footnote is nearly a page long. I felt that two sentences of main text and a page of footnotes were too much.' A glance at the first volume of *Das Kapital* exposes this as a wild exaggeration: there are indeed several footnotes in the opening pages, but none of more than a few sentences. Nevertheless, Wilson probably spoke for many other readers who have been put off by the perceived or actual 'difficulty' of the book.

Marx anticipated this reaction in his preface. 'The understanding of the first chapter, especially the section that contains the analysis of commodities, will... present the greatest difficulty. I have popularized the passages concerning the substance of value and the magnitude of value as much as possible.' The value-form, he claimed, was simplicity itself. 'Nevertheless, the human mind has laboured for more than 2,000 years to get to the bottom of it... With the exception of the section on the form of value, therefore, this volume cannot stand accused on the score of difficulty. I assume, of course, a reader who is willing to learn something new and therefore to think for himself.'

Even Engels was unconvinced. While the book was being typeset he warned Marx that it was a serious mistake not to clarify the theoretical arguments by splitting them into shorter sections with separate headings. 'The thing would have looked somewhat like a school textbook, but a very large class of readers would have found it considerably easier to understand. The *populus,* even the scholars, just are no longer at all accustomed to this way of thinking, and one has to make it as easy for them as one possibly can.' Marx did make some changes to the proof sheets, but they were no more than marginal tinkerings. 'How could you leave the *outward* structure of the book in its present form!' Engels asked despairingly after seeing the final proofs. 'The fourth chapter is almost 200 pages long and only has four sub-sections... Furthermore, the train of thought is constantly interrupted by illustrations, and the point to be illustrated is *never* summarized after the illustration, so that one is forever plunging straight from the illustration of *one* point into the exposition of another point. It is dreadfully tiring, and confusing, too.'

Other admirers also found their eyes glazing over as they wrestled with the obscure early chapters. 'Please be so good as to tell your wife,' Marx wrote to Ludwig Kugelmann, the friend in Hanover, 'that the chapters on "The Working Day", "Co-operation, Division of Labour and Machinery" and finally on "Primitive Accumulation" are the most immediately readable. You will have to explain any incomprehensible terminology to her. If there are any other doubtful points, I shall be glad to help.' When the great English socialist William Morris read Das Kapital, he 'thoroughly enjoyed the historical part' but confessed to suffering 'agonies of confusion of the brain over reading the pure economics of that great work. Anyway, I read what I could, and will hope that some information stuck to me from my reading.' (It proved a good investment in every sense: Morris's copy of the first volume, in a gorgeously ornate leather binding, was sold at auction for $50,000 in May 1989.)

Sheer incomprehension, rather than political enmity, may explain the muted reaction to Das Kapital on its first publication. 'The silence about my book makes me fidgety,' Marx fretted. Engels tried to stir up publicity by submitting hostile pseudonymous reviews to German newspapers and urged Marx's other friends to do likewise. 'The main thing is that the book should be discussed over and over again, in any way whatsoever,' he told Kugelmann. 'In the words of our old friend Jesus Christ, we must be as innocent as doves and wise as serpents.' Kugelmann did his best, placing articles in a couple of Hanover papers, but since he barely understood the book himself they were none too illuminating. 'Kugelmann becomes more simple-minded every day,' Engels fumed.

It took four years for the 1,000 copies of the first edition to sell out. Although Marx claimed in his afterword to the second edition (1872) that 'the appreciation which Das Kapital rapidly gained in wide circles of the German working class is the best reward for my labours', it seems unlikely that the

volume reached many workers – though they were introduced to its main themes in a series of articles by Joseph
Dietzgen for the socialist *Demokratisches Wochenblatt*. 'There
can be few books that have been written in more difficult circumstances,' Jenny Marx wrote. 'If the workers had an inkling
of the sacrifices that were necessary for this work, which was
written only for them and for their sakes, to be completed,
they would perhaps show a little more interest.' But how
could they, given its length and density and unfamiliar subject? As Marx himself pointed out, 'political economy remains
a foreign science in Germany'.

Elsewhere, however, there were stirrings of interest. As
early as January 1868, two months after publication, the
London *Saturday Review* included *Das Kapital* in a round-up of
recent German books. 'The author's views may be as perni-
cious as we conceive them to be,' it concluded, 'but there can
be no question as to the plausibility of his logic, the vigour of
his rhetoric, and the charm with which he invests the driest
problems of political economy.' A notice in the *Contemporary
Review* five months later, while patriotically scornful of
German economics ('we do not suspect that Karl Marx has
much to teach us'), complimented the author on not forget-
ting 'the human interest – the "hunger and thirst interest"
which underlies the science'.

A Russian translation of *Das Kapital* appeared in the spring
of 1872, passed by the Tsar's censors on the grounds that it
had no application to Russia and therefore couldn't be subversive (though they did remove a picture of the author,

fearing that it might inspire a personality cult). They judged the text so impenetrable that 'few would read it and still fewer understand it', but most of the 3,000 print run was sold within a year. While his book was unobtainable and unknown in most capitalist countries of the West, newspapers and journals in pre-capitalist Russia were running favourable reviews. 'Isn't it an irony of fate,' Marx wrote to Engels, 'that the Russians, whom I have fought for twenty-five years, always want to be my patrons? They run after the most extreme ideas the West has to offer, out of pure gluttony.' He was specially gratified by a notice in the *St Petersburg Journal*, praising the 'unusual liveliness' of his prose. 'In this respect,' it added, 'the author in no way resembles… the majority of German scholars, who… write their books in a language so dry and obscure that the heads of ordinary mortals are cracked by it.'

The production of a French edition was more problematic. Although work began in 1867, immediately after German publication, over the next four years no fewer than five translators were tried and rejected. Eventually Marx gave his blessing to a Bordeaux schoolteacher, Joseph Roy. After inspecting the early chapters, however, he decided that although they were 'well done on the whole', Roy had often translated too literally. 'I have therefore found myself compelled to rewrite whole passages in French, to make them palatable.' With Marx's approval, the publisher decided to issue the book in instalments ('more easily accessible to the working class'), the first of which appeared in May 1875.

In his adopted country, those promising early reviews were followed by a long silence. 'Though Marx has lived much in England,' the barrister Sir John MacDonnell wrote in the *Fortnightly Review* in March 1875, 'he is here almost the shadow of a name. People may do him the honour of abusing him; read him they do not.' Marx believed that 'the peculiar gift of stolid blockheadedness' was every Briton's birthright, and the fact that no English edition was available in his lifetime confirmed his prejudice. 'We are much obliged by your letter,' Messrs Macmillan & Co. wrote to Engels's friend Carl Schorlemmer, the professor of organic chemistry at Manchester University, 'but we are not disposed to entertain the publication of a translation of *Das Kapital*.' Those few Britons who wanted to study it had to struggle as best they could with the German, Russian or French versions. The radical English journalist Peter Fox, publisher of the *National Reformer*, said after being presented with the German edition that he felt like a man who had acquired an elephant and didn't know what to do with it. A working-class Scotsman, Robert Banner, sent Marx this anguished appeal for help:

> Is there no hope of it being translated? There is no work to be had in English advocating the cause of the toiling masses, every book we young Socialists put our hands on is work in the interest of Capital, hence the backwardness of our cause in this country. With a work dealing with economics from the standpoint of Socialism, you would soon see a movement

in this country that would put the nightcap on this bastard
thing.

Those most in need of the book were the least able to understand it, while the educated elite who could read it had no
wish to do so. As the English socialist Henry Hyndman
wrote: 'Accustomed as we are nowadays, especially in
England, to fence always with big soft buttons on the point of
our rapiers, Marx's terrible onslaught with naked steel upon
his adversaries appeared so improper that it was impossible
for our gentlemanly sham-fighters and mental gymnasium
men to believe that this unsparing controversialist and furious assailant of capital and capitalism was really the deepest
thinker of our times.'

Hyndman himself was an exception to the rule. Early in
1880, after reading the French translation of *Das Kapital*, he
bombarded the author with so many extravagant tributes that
Marx felt obliged to meet him. But although Hyndman pro-
fessed himself 'eager to learn', it was he who did most of the
talking: Marx came to dread the visits from this 'complacent
chatterbox'. Their inevitable rupture occurred in June 1881,
when Hyndman's socialist manifesto *England for All* included
two chapters largely plagiarized from *Das Kapital* without
permission or even acknowledgement – save for a note in the
preface admitting that 'for the ideas and much of the matter
contained in Chapters II and III, I am indebted to the work of
a great thinker and original writer, which will, I trust, shortly
be made accessible to the majority of my countrymen'. Marx

thought this shamefully inadequate: why not mention *Das Kapital* or its author by name? Hyndman's limp excuse was that the English had 'a horror of socialism' and 'a dread of being taught by a foreigner'. As Marx pointed out, however, the book was unlikely to assuage that horror by evoking 'the dream of socialism' on page 86, and any half-intelligent reader would surely guess from the preface that the anonymous 'great thinker' must be foreign. It was larceny, pure and simple – compounded by the insertion of imbecilic errors in the few paragraphs that were not lifted verbatim from *Das Kapital*.

No sooner had Marx fallen out with one English disciple than he acquired another – though this time he took the precaution of never meeting the man. Ernest Belfort Bax, born in 1854, had been radicalized by the Paris Commune while still a schoolboy, and in 1879 began a long series of articles for the highbrow monthly *Modern Thought* on the intellectual titans of the age, including Schopenhauer, Wagner and (in 1881) Karl Marx. Having studied Hegelian philosophy in Germany, Bax was probably the only English socialist of his generation to accept the dialectic as the inner dynamic of life. He described *Das Kapital* as a book 'that embodies the working out of a doctrine in economy comparable in its revolutionary character and wide-reaching importance to the Copernican system in astronomy, or the law of gravitation in Mechanics'. Marx was understandably delighted, hailing Bax's article as 'the first publication of that kind which is pervaded by a real enthusiasm for the new ideas themselves and boldly stands up against British philistinism'.

For all his faults, however, the despised Hyndman did more than Bax or anyone else to spread Marx's ideas in this philistine nation. He remained a fervent disciple, quoting Marx at length – and by name this time – in his 1883 book, *The Historical Basis of Socialism in England.* He even founded an explicitly Marxist political party, the Democratic Federation (later the Social Democratic Federation), whose leading members included Bax, William Morris, Walter Crane, Marx's own daughter, Eleanor, and her lover, Edward Aveling. Hyndman's enthusiastic advocacy of *Das Kapital* at meetings of the Federation prompted the young Irish writer George Bernard Shaw to spend the autumn of 1883 studying the French edition in the British Museum reading room, where Marx himself had quarried much of the raw material. 'That was the turning point in my career,' Shaw recalled. 'Marx was a revelation... He opened my eyes to the facts of history and civilization, gave me an entirely fresh conception of the universe, provided me with a purpose and a mission in life.' *Das Kapital,* he wrote, 'achieved the greatest feat of which a book is capable – that of changing the minds of the people who read it'.

Shaw's passion for *Das Kapital* never dimmed, as he proved with this characteristically extravagant tribute on the very first page of *Everybody's Political What's What,* written more than sixty years later:

Not until the nineteenth century, when Karl Marx tore the

reports of our factory inspectors from our unread Blue
Books and revealed capitalism in all its atrocity, did
Pessimism and Cynicism reach their blackest depth. He
proved up to the hilt that capital in its pursuit of what he
called *Mehrwerth,* which we translate as Surplus Value (it
includes rent, interest and commercial profit), is ruthless,
and will stop at nothing, not even at mutilation and
massacre, white and black slavery, drugging and drinking,
if they promise a shilling per cent more than the dividends
of philanthropy. Before Marx there had been plenty of
Pessimism. The book of Ecclesiastes in the Bible is full of it.
Shakespeare in *King Lear,* in *Timon of Athens,* in *Coriolanus,*
got to it and stuck there. So did Swift and Goldsmith. But
none of them could document the case from official sources
as Marx did. He thereby created that demand for 'a new
world' which not only inspires modern Communism and
Socialism but in 1941 became the platform catchword of
zealous Conservatives and Churchmen.

Shaw had little success in spreading the gospel to fellow
members of the Fabian Society, which he joined in 1884. His
friend H. G. Wells dismissed Marx as 'a stuffy, ego-centred
and malicious theorist' who 'offered to the cheapest and
basest of human impulses the poses of a pretentious philosophy'. Under the influence of their chief theorist, Sidney Webb,
the Fabians guided British socialism away from notions of
class war and revolution into the belief that, with universal
suffrage, the existing British state could enact social legisla-

tion to improve the welfare of the working class and the efficiency of the economic system. This also became the dominant credo of the Labour Party, formed in 1900. The old quip that Labour owed more to Methodism than to Marx may be an exaggeration: its supporters, and its Members of Parliament, have included many socialists who might call themselves Marxians if not Marxists; in 1947 the party even issued a reprint of the *Communist Manifesto* to 'acknowledge its indebtedness to Marx and Engels as two men who have been the inspiration of the whole working-class movement'. But Labour leaders have consistently upheld Harold Wilson's view that Marx's legacy is irrelevant, perhaps actually inimical, to a constitutional party of the centre-left.

In Germany, Marx's homeland, his ideas became the ruling ideology of the Sozialistische Partei Deutschlands (SPD) at its 1891 congress in Erfurt. But the Erfurt programme had two distinct halves, presaging a long struggle between revolutionaries and revisionists. The first section, drafted by Marx's disciple Karl Kautsky, restated theories familiar from *Das Kapital*, such as the tendency to monopoly and the immiseration of the proletariat; the second half, written by Eduard Bernstein, dealt with more immediate political objectives – universal suffrage, free education, a progressive income tax. Bernstein had lived in London during the 1880s and fallen under the influence of the early Fabians: Rosa Luxemburg complained that he 'sees the world through English spectacles'.

Bernstein openly repudiated much of Marx's legacy in the

decade after the Erfurt congress, dismissing his theory of value as 'a purely abstract concept' which failed to explain the relationship between supply and demand. Kautsky was at first reluctant to criticize his old comrade, sometimes seeming even to encourage him: 'You have overthrown our tactics, our theory of value, our philosophy; now all depends on what is the new that you are thinking of putting in place of the old.' By the end of the century, Bernstein's intentions were all too apparent. Capitalism, far from being overthrown by an inevitable and imminent crisis, would probably endure and bring increased prosperity to the masses. If properly regulated, it might actually prove to be the engine of social progress:

> It is thus quite wrong to assume that the present development of society shows a relative or indeed absolute diminution of the number of the members of the possessing classes. Their number increases both relatively and absolutely… The prospects of socialism depend not on the decrease but on the increase of social wealth.

Although the SPD continued to define itself as a revolutionary proletarian organization, in practice it became an increasingly successful parliamentary party led by gradualists and technocrats.

As a connoisseur of irony, even Marx might have been obliged to smile (or at least grimace) at his fate: a prophet without much honour in his own land, still less in his adopted home of Britain, he became the inspiration for a cataclysmic upheaval in the place where he least expected it – Russia, a nation scarcely mentioned in *Das Kapital*. Yet by the end of his life he had already begun to regret the omission: the success of the Russian edition of *Das Kapital* set him wondering if perhaps there was some revolutionary potential there after all.

His translator in St Petersburg, Nikolai Danielson, was also the leader of the Narodnik movement, which believed that Russia could go straight from feudalism to socialism. Marx's portrait of capitalism's soul-destroying effects convinced them that this stage of economic evolution should be avoided if at all possible, and since Russia already had an embryonic form of common land ownership in the countryside it would be perverse to break up peasant communes and hand them over to private landlords merely for the sake of obeying some allegedly ineluctable historical law. For more orthodox Marxists such as Georgy Plekhanov, who maintained that conditions for socialism would not ripen until Russia had industrialized, this was self-deluding folly – and for a decade or so after *Das Kapital*'s appearance Marx seemed to think so too. Replying in 1877 to a Narodnik who protested at his determinist view of history, he wrote that if Russia was to become a capitalist nation after the example of Western European countries 'she will not succeed without having first transformed a good part of her peasants into proletarians; and after that, once taken to the bosom of the capitalist regime, she will experience its pitiless laws like other profane peoples'.

Yet Marx continued to brood on developments in Russia, which threatened to disprove his theories. The insurrectionary movement might be small but it was awesomely determined and effective: between 1879 and 1881 a breakaway faction of Narodniks, The People's Will, staged seven attempts on the life of Tsar Alexander II, the last of which succeeded. (Six years later The People's Will also tried to assassinate Tsar Alexander III; one of those hanged for his part in the plot was Alexander Ulyanov, whose teenage brother Vladimir Ilich Ulyanov would become better known as V. I. Lenin.) The ensuing spate of arrests and executions drove many Russian revolutionaries into exile. Plekhanov moved to Switzerland with several comrades including Vera Zasulich, who in 1876 had shot the governor-general of St Petersburg and then given such a virtuoso courtroom performance that a jury acquitted her of attempted murder. Despite her record, she disapproved of the increasingly violent, regicidal trend in Russian socialism, which seemed to have lost sight of the economic imperatives laid down in *Das Kapital*. But the question of peasants and proletarians continued to trouble Zasulich and her fellow exiles on the shores of Lake Geneva. In February 1881 she appealed to Marx for an authoritative opinion. 'You are not unaware that your *Kapital* is enjoying great popularity in Russia,' she wrote. 'But what you probably do not know is the role which your *Kapital* plays in our discussion of the agrarian question.' Could he please settle the dispute 'by conveying your ideas on the possible future of our rural commune and the theory of the historical inevitability for all countries of the world to pass through all phases of capitalist production'?

Marx agonized over the problem for several weeks, writing no fewer than five drafts of his reply. Eventually he sent her a brief letter saying that his 'so-called theory' had been misunderstood: the historical inevitability of the bourgeois phase 'is *expressly* limited to the *countries of Western Europe*'. The Western transition from feudalism to capitalism represented the transformation of one type of private property into another, whereas in the case of the Russian peasants 'their communal property would, on the contrary, have to be transformed into private property. Hence the analysis provided in *Das Kapital* does not adduce reasons either for or against the viability of the rural commune.' This was more encouraging than his comments of only four years earlier – but far more cautious than the first draft of his letter to Zasulich, which explained why and how the Russian peasantry could escape the fate of its Western European counterparts:

In Russia, thanks to a unique combination of circumstances, the rural commune, still established on a nationwide scale, may gradually detach itself from its primitive features and develop directly as an element of collective production on a nationwide scale… To save the Russian commune, a Russian revolution is needed. For that matter, the government and the 'new pillars of society' are doing their best to prepare the masses for just such a disaster. If revolution comes at the opportune moment, if it concentrates all its forces so as to

allow the rural commune full scope, the latter will soon
develop as an element of regeneration in Russian society and
an element of superiority over the countries enslaved by the
capitalist system.

Five days after Marx sent his final version, a small group from
The People's Will assassinated Tsar Alexander II in St Petersburg by throwing a bomb at his coach.

With his long-held conviction that revolution could be
achieved only through collective action by the working class,
rather than by individual stunts or acts of terrorism, Marx
might have been expected to side with Zasulich and
Plekhanov rather than the death-or-glory bombers. In a letter
to his daughter Jenny, however, he confided that the Swiss
exiles were 'mere doctrinaires, muddle-headed anarcho-
socialists, and their influence on the Russian "theatre of war"
is zero'. The St Petersburg assassins, by contrast, 'are sterling
chaps through and through, without melodramatic postur-
ing, simple, matter-of-fact, heroic… They are at pains to teach
Europe that their *modus operandi* is a specifically Russian and
historically inevitable mode of action which no more lends
itself to moralizing – for or against – than does the earthquake
in Chios.'

It is inconceivable that a younger Karl Marx would have
taken such an attitude: he had spent many years denouncing
socialists who put their trust in *coups, attentats* and clandes-
tine conspiracies. By 1881, however, he was ill and exhausted.
Having waited so long for a proper proletarian revolution he

now seemed wearily impatient for an uprising of any kind. Following the birth of a grandson that spring, he mused that children 'born at this turning point of history… have before them the most revolutionary period men had ever to pass through. The bad thing now is to be "old" so as to be only able to foresee instead of seeing.'

The architects of the 1917 revolution all cited Marx, and *Das Kapital* in particular, as the divine authority for the correctness of their views. Trotsky had studied the book in 1900 while exiled to a ghastly insect-infested village in Siberia – 'brushing the cockroaches off the pages', as he recalled. Lenin claimed to have read it in 1888, at the precocious age of eighteen, sitting on an old stove in the kitchen at his grandfather's apartment. Thereafter he used *Das Kapital* – or those parts that suited his purposes – as a blade with which to slash his rivals. (Maxim Gorky said of Lenin's speeches that they had 'the cold glitter of steel shavings'.) Although his first major work, *The Development of Capitalism in Russia*, was presented as a sort of supplement to Marx, it had none of *Das Kapital*'s irony and indignation. As Edmund Wilson remarked, 'All the writing of Lenin is functional; it is all aimed at accomplishing an immediate purpose… He is simply a man who wants to convince.' The immediate purpose of *The Development of Capitalism in Russia* was to persuade his comrades that their country had already emerged from feudalism thanks to the rapid spread of railways, coal mines, steel mills and textile factories in the 1880s and 1890s. True, an industrial proletariat existed only in Moscow and St Petersburg, but this strengthened its duty to act as a vanguard class expressing the grievances of peasants and artisans elsewhere. In the new factories, he wrote, 'exploitation is fully developed and emerges in its pure form, without any confusing details. The worker cannot fail to see that he is oppressed by capital... That is why the factory worker is none other than the foremost representative of the entire exploited population.' But in his later tract *What Is To Be Done?* he added that the workers were too preoccupied with their own economic struggle to develop a true revolutionary consciousness:

> There is much talk of spontaneity. But the spontaneous development of the working-class movement leads to its subordination to bourgeois ideology; for the spontaneous working-class movement is trade unionism, and trade unionism means the ideological enslavement of the workers by the bourgeoisie. Hence our task, the task of Social Democracy, is to combat spontaneity, to divert the working-class movement from this spontaneous, trade unionist striving to come under the wing of the bourgeoisie, and to bring it under the wing of revolutionary Social Democracy.

Mass campaigns for better conditions and shorter working weeks, advocated by Marx in *Das Kapital*, were dismissed by Lenin as a waste of time. Instead, the workers should place themselves at the disposal of professional revolutionaries such as himself: 'The contemporary socialist movement can come into being only on the basis of a profound scientific knowledge... The bearer of this science is not the proletariat but the bourgeois intelligentsia.' In these sentences one can see in embryonic form what eventually became a monstrous tyranny.

As the self-appointed bearer of the Ten Commandments, Lenin liked to remind comrades of their lowlier intellectual status. 'It is impossible to understand Marx's *Das Kapital* and especially its first chapters without having thoroughly studied and understood the *whole* of Hegel's *Logic*,' he wrote in his *Philosophical Notebooks.* 'Consequently, half a century later, none of the Marxists understands Marx.' Except him, of course. Yet for all his reading and writing, Lenin's own 'scientific knowledge' was no more profound than it needed to be. Here is an acute assessment by Trotsky, who observed him as closely as anyone:

> The whole of Marx appears in the *Communist Manifesto*, in the *Critique of Political Economy*, in *Das Kapital*. Even if he had never been destined to become the founder of the First International, he would still remain for all times the figure which we know today. The whole of Lenin on the other hand appears in revolutionary action. His scientific works are only a preliminary for activity.

And perhaps not even a preliminary. 'The seizure of power,' Lenin wrote in 1917, 'is the point of the uprising. Its political task will be clarified after the seizure.' As the historian Bertram Wolfe points out, this turns Marx on his head: the

Marxist belief that ultimately economics determines politics 'becomes the Leninist view that, with enough determination, power itself, naked political power, might succeed wholly in determining economics'. No wonder the prevailing creed of the Soviet Union acquired the name Marxism-Leninism, rather than simple Marxism. Marx's favourite motto was *de omnibus dubitandum* ('everything should be questioned'), but no one who tried to practise this in Communist Russia survived for long. Marxism as practised by Marx himself was not so much an ideology as a critical process, a continuous dialectical argument; Lenin and then Stalin froze it into dogma. (As, of course, had other socialists before them. 'The Social Democratic Federation here shares with your German-American Socialists the distinction of being the only parties who have contrived to reduce the Marxist theory of development to a rigid orthodoxy,' Engels complained to Friedrich Adolph Sorge, a German émigré in New York, in May 1894. 'This theory is to be forced down the throats of the workers at once and without development as articles of faith, instead of making the workers raise themselves to its level by dint of their own class instinct. That is why both remain mere sects and, as Hegel says, come from nothing through nothing to nothing.') One could even argue that the most truly Marxist achievement of the Soviet Union was its collapse: a centralized, secretive and bureaucratic command economy proved incompatible with new forces of production, thus precipitating a change in the relations of production. Mikhail Gorbachev admitted as much in his 1987 book, *Perestroika:*

The management system which took shape in the thirties and forties began gradually to contradict the demands and conditions of economic progress. Its positive potential was exhausted. It became more and more of a hindrance, and gave rise to the braking mechanism which did us so much harm later…

It was in these conditions that a prejudiced attitude to the role of commodity-monetary relations and the law of value under socialism developed, and the claim was often made that they were opposite and alien to socialism. All this was combined with an underestimation of profit-and-loss accounting, and produced disarray in pricing, and a disregard for the circulation of money… Ever increasing signs appeared of man's alienation from the property of the whole people, of lack of coordination between public interest and the personal interests of the working person.

After Russia, the next major country to proclaim itself Communist was China, which became a 'People's Republic' in 1949. Whereas Marx and Lenin had focused on the urban proletariat, Mao Zedong argued that rural peasants could be a revolutionary force if guided by 'correct' leaders such as himself. Shunning the Soviet model of urgent industrialization, he made rural development the top priority, thus inspiring many Marxists in Third-World countries which had no industry worth the name. But the Maoist programme was a disaster for the Chinese peasantry: the Great Leap Forward, a scheme to collectivize agriculture and promote small-scale rural industries, brought mass starvation in its wake and was abandoned in 1960 only two years after its inception. This coincided with a rupture between China and the Soviet Union, as Nikita Khrushchev ridiculed the Great Leap and Mao retaliated by denouncing him as a 'capitalist roader'. Since the Great Helmsman's death in 1976, however, China has itself set off down the capitalist route, becoming the world's most rapidly growing industrial economy while still maintaining that it has in fact now reached 'the primary stage of socialism'. Despite having abandoned all Mao's precepts, the government in Beijing continues to define itself as Marxist-Leninist, though 'Market-Leninist' would be rather more apt.

Like Christianity with its countless rival sects, Marxism has appeared in many strikingly different and apparently incongruous guises – Bolsheviks and Mensheviks, Spartacists and revisionists, Stalinists and Trotskyists, Maoists and Castroites, Eurocommunists and existentialists. Marx himself had foreseen, with grim resignation, that his name would be taken in vain by 'Marxists' long after he was dead and in no position to protest. His most famous expression of despair at deluded disciples was a rebuke to French socialists in the 1870s: if they were Marxists, he sighed, 'all I know is that I am not a Marxist'. And perhaps he wasn't. The history of the twentieth century revealed that Marxist revolution was most likely in countries which did not have an advanced industrial economy, a capitalist class or a large army of wage-earning proletarians. Hence the paradox noted by the Marxian scholar

David McLellan in 1983, when almost half the world was still ruled by regimes claiming to be Marx's heirs:

> The very fact that Marxism has not triumphed in the West means that it has not been turned into an official ideology and is thus the object of serious study unimpeded by government controls. It is precisely in Western Europe and America – the capitalist countries – that Marx is studied most carefully. Indeed, it is fair to say that there are more real Marxists in the West than in many of the so-called 'Marxist' countries.

In Communist states from Albania to Zimbabwe, the local definition of Marxism was laid down by the government and no further discussion was required (or indeed permitted). In the West, however, its meaning became the object of both strident argument and subtle reassessment. The work of the so-called Frankfurt school in the 1930s – including Max Horkheimer, Theodor Adorno and Herbert Marcuse – gave rise to a new breed of Marxist philosophy known as 'critical theory', which rejected the economic determinism of Lenin and the Bolsheviks. The Frankfurt school, and other thinkers of the period such as Antonio Gramsci, also questioned traditional Marxist attitudes to proletarian class consciousness. Capitalism, according to Gramsci, maintained its hegemony by deluding or bullying the working class into an acceptance of bourgeois culture as the norm, empowering certain values and practices while excluding others. To challenge this consensus and explode its pretensions, the workers must develop a 'counter-hegemonic' culture of their own through new systems of popular education.

Western Marxists therefore placed far greater emphasis on the importance of what Marx called superstructure – culture, institutions, language – in the political process, so much so that consideration of the economic base sometimes disappeared altogether. Unable to change the world, they concentrated on interpreting it through what became known as 'cultural studies' – which established its own hegemony on many university campuses in the final decades of the twentieth century, transforming the study of history, geography, sociology, anthropology and literature. Even the libido was subjected to Marxist scrutiny. The psychiatrist Wilhelm Reich tried to reconcile Marx and Freud by proposing that the workers couldn't be truly free until they were liberated from sexual repression and the tyranny of traditional family structures (though Marx himself had dismissed free love as a 'bestial' prospect, tantamount to 'general prostitution'). 'Sex is integrated into work and public relations and thus is made more susceptible to (controlled) satisfaction,' wrote Herbert Marcuse, a guru of the New Left, in *One-Dimensional Man* (1964). 'Technical progress and more comfortable living permit the systematic inclusion of libidinal components into the realm of commodity production and exchange.'

That realm was defined far more broadly than Marx ever imagined. It encompassed any and every sort of cultural commodity – a pair of winklepicker shoes, a newspaper photograph, a pop record and a packet of breakfast cereal were all 'texts' that could be 'read'. The critique of mass culture from early theorists influenced by the Frankfurt school was gradually supplanted by a study of the different ways in which people receive and interpret these everyday texts. As cultural studies took a 'linguistic turn' – evolving through structuralism, post-structuralism, deconstruction and then postmodernism – it often seemed a way of evading politics altogether, even though many of its practitioners continued to call themselves Marxists. The logic of their playful insistence that there were no certainties or realities led ultimately to a free-floating, value-free relativism which could celebrate both American pop culture and medieval superstition without a qualm. Despite their scorn for grand historical narratives and general laws of nature, many seemed to accept the enduring success of capitalism as an immutable fact of life. Their subversive impulses sought refuge in marginal spaces where the victors' dominance seemed less secure: hence their enthusiasm for the exotic and unincorporable, from UFO conspiracy theories to sado-masochistic fetishes. A fascination with the pleasures of consumption (TV soap operas, shopping malls, mass-market kitsch) displaced the traditional Marxist focus on the conditions of material production. The consequence was, in the words of the Marxist critic Terry Eagleton, 'an immense linguistic inflation, as what appeared no longer conceivable in political reality was still just about possible in the areas of discourse or signs or textuality. The freedom of text or language would come to compensate for the unfreedom of the system as a whole.' The new enemy, Eagleton writes, was 'coherent belief systems of any kind – in particular all forms of political theory and organization which sought to analyse, and act upon, the structures of society as a whole. For it was precisely such politics which seemed to have failed.' No systematic critique of monopoly capitalism could be achieved since capitalism was itself a fiction, like truth, justice, law and all other 'linguistic constructs'.

Where, one might wonder, did this leave Karl Marx, who had striven to produce just such a systematic critique? While happily deconstructing TV commercials or sweet-wrappers, theorists seemed curiously reluctant to take their scalpels to the text of *Das Kapital*, perhaps for fear of committing literary parricide. The postmodernist historian Dominick LaCapra says it is 'probably the most crying case of a canonical text in need of rereading rather than straightforward, literal reading geared to a purely unitary authorial voice'.

The most notable reassessment in this vein is *Reading 'Capital'* (1965), a collection of essays by Louis Althusser and some of his students, which begins with this statement of intent:

> Of course, we have all read, and all do read *'Capital'*. For almost a century, we have been able to read it every day, transparently, in the dramas and dreams of our history, in its disputes and conflicts, in the defeats and victories of the workers' movement which is our only hope and our destiny. Since we 'came into the world', we have read *'Capital'* constantly in the writings and speeches of those

who have read it for us, well or ill, both the dead and
the living, Engels, Kautsky, Plekhanov, Lenin, Rosa
Luxemburg, Trotsky, Stalin, Gramsci, the leaders of the
workers' organizations, their supporters and opponents:
philosophers, economists, politicians. We have read bits of
it, the 'fragments' which the conjuncture had 'selected' for
us. We have even all, more or less, read Volume One, from
'commodities' to the 'expropriation of the expropriators'.

But some day it is essential to read *'Capital'* to the letter.
To read the text itself...

Althusser, like any reader, comes to this assignment wearing
a pair of spectacles that conform to his own prescription. It
was he who first insisted that there was an unbridgeable gulf
– an 'epistemological break' – between the Marx of the 1840s
and the man who wrote *Das Kapital* twenty years later. In contrast to Jean-Paul Sartre, who found rich inspiration in the
early philosophical writings for his formulation of Marxism
as a history of human self-emancipation, Althusser deplored
the younger Marx's interest in ethics, alienation and 'human
agency'. To Althusser, history was a 'process without a subject' and therefore unworthy of study or analysis: individuals,
even collectively, could never escape or challenge the imper-
sonal forces of the Ideological State Apparatus – education,
religion, the family – which produce and maintain the dominant belief system.

Althusser rescued Marx from the narrow economic determinism imposed by Lenin and his heirs only to confine him in

an equally restrictive straitjacket. In *Reading 'Capital'* he reduced Marx's *magnum opus* to a purely scientific work, unsullied by Hegelian influence – despite the author's own cheerful acknowledgement of the debt, particularly in the opening chapter on commodities. Marxism became nothing more than a theory of structural practices, divorced from politics, history and experience.

The logic of Althusser's anti-humanism was that people could not be held responsible for their actions – a contention he himself exploited years later to absolve himself from any guilt after murdering his wife. On a grander scale, it served to exculpate the Communist Party (of which he was a long-standing member): mass murder in the Soviet Union was not a crime, merely a theoretical error – or, in Althusser's hideous euphemism for Stalinism, 'that new form of "non-rational existence of reason"'. As the Marxist historian E. P. Thompson wrote in his spirited polemic *The Poverty of Theory* (1979): 'We can see the emergence of Althusserianism as a manifestation of a general police action within ideology, as the attempt to reconstruct Stalinism at the level of theory.' He added that Althusser's insistence on a wholly conceptual Marxism, uncontaminated by history or experience, exposed him as a man 'who has only a casual acquaintance with historical practice' – for in the real world, time and again, 'experience walks in without knocking at the door and announces deaths and crises of substance'. This was more accurate than Thompson realized. The full extent of Althusser's ignorance was laid bare in his posthumous memoir, *The Future Lasts Forever* (1994), where he confessed to being 'a trickster and a deceiver' who sometimes invented quotations to suit his purposes. 'In fact, my philosophical knowledge of texts was rather limited. I... knew a little Spinoza, nothing about Aristotle, the Sophists and the Stoics, quite a lot about Plato and Pascal, nothing about Kant, a bit about Hegel, and finally a few passages of Marx.'

How did he get away with it? His explanation of the conjuring trick is startlingly candid:

> I had another particular ability. Starting from a simple turn of phrase, I thought I could work out (what an illusion!), if not the specific ideas of an author or a book I had not read, at least their general drift or direction. I obviously had certain intuitive powers as well as a definite ability for seeing connections, or a capacity for establishing theoretical oppositions, which enabled me to reconstruct what I took to be an author's ideas on the basis of the authors to whom he was opposed. I proceeded spontaneously by drawing contrasts and distinctions, subsequently elaborating a theory to support this.

Thanks to these intuitive powers, *Reading 'Capital'* is illuminated by occasional flashes of insight even though Althusser had studied only a few passages of Marx. He proposes that *Das Kapital* should be seen as 'an important answer to a *question that is nowhere posed*, an answer which Marx only succeeds in formulating on condition of multiplying the images required to render it… The age Marx lived in did not provide him, and he could not acquire in his lifetime, an adequate concept with which to think what he produced: *the concept of the effectivity of a structure on its elements.*'

Marx, in other words, had fashioned a delayed-action booby-trap, waiting for someone to ask the question which he had already answered. This is borne out by a letter he sent to Engels soon after the completion of the first volume in 1867, predicting the objections of 'vulgar economists' to *Das Kapital:* 'If I wished to refute all such objections *in advance,* I should spoil the whole dialectical method of exposition. On the contrary, the good thing about this method is that it is constantly setting traps for those fellows which will provoke them into an untimely display of their idiocy.' Again, one cannot help recalling the ironic sting of Balzac's *Unknown Masterpiece*: the only failing of the painter's blotchy, formless and seemingly disastrous masterwork was that he executed it a hundred years too soon, since it was in fact a piece of twentieth-century abstract art. As Edmund Wilson wrote, by championing the dispossessed classes and laying siege to the fortress of bourgeois self-satisfaction, Marx brought into economics a point of view 'which was of value to his time precisely in proportion as it was alien to it'.

For half a century after *Das Kapital*'s publication, however, vulgar economists showed little interest in refuting Marx, preferring to ignore him. They saw the capitalist system as a permanent necessity, rather than a passing historical phase which contained within it the germs of its own terminal illness. Whereas Marx treated interest and profit and rent as unpaid labour, academic economists described the interest obtained by capital-owners as 'the reward of abstinence'. For Alfred Marshall, the dominant figure in British economics during the late-Victorian and Edwardian eras, those who accumulate capital rather than spending it are performing a 'sacrifice of waiting', and therefore deserve compensation for their virtuous restraint.

Orthodox economics held that over-production, which Marx regarded as an essential feature of capitalism, simply could not occur. According to Say's Law of Markets, supply created its own demand: earnings from the production and sale of certain commodities provided the purchasing power to buy others. This same self-righting mechanism ensured that unemployment could never be more than a brief, accidental blemish. Unemployed people would be willing to work for lower pay; the consequent fall in wages would lower the price of the commodities they produced, which in turn would raise demand for the goods and increase their sales, thus enabling full employment to resume.

The economic turbulence and heavy unemployment between the two World Wars forced a reconsideration, and a belated acknowledgement that capitalism might have systematic defects after all. Some economists even began to question if it really was eternal and immutable. In his 1939 study, *Value and Capital,* Professor John Hicks doubted that 'one could count upon the long survival of anything like a capitalist system' in the absence of new inventions strong enough to maintain investment. 'One cannot repress the thought,' he added, 'that perhaps the whole Industrial Revolution of the last two hundred years has been nothing but a vast secular boom.' J. M. Keynes, born in the year of Marx's death, wrote in his *General Theory of Employment, Interest and Money* (1936): 'I see the *rentier* aspect of capitalism as a transitional phase which will disappear when it has done its work.'

Keynes, the most influential economist of the twentieth century, challenged the notion that *laissez-faire* capitalism had a natural tendency to self-equilibrium. The idea that unemployment forced down wages and thereby restored full employment might be true in individual companies or industries. But if *all* wages were cut, then *all* incomes would fall and demand would stagnate, giving employers no incentive to hire more labour. In the words of the Keynesian economist Joan Robinson, 'In a crowd, anyone can get a better view of the procession if he stands on a chair. But if they all get up on chairs no one has a better view.'

Before Keynes, most economists treated capitalism's occasional crises as negligible aberrations. He saw them as the inescapable rhythm of an unstable system – just as Marx had. Yet Keynes dismissed Marx as a crank from 'the underworld of economic thought', whose theories were 'illogical, obsolete, scientifically erroneous, and without interest or application to the modern world'. The vehemence of his denunciation is surprising, given the resemblance between Marx's critique of classical economists and Keynes's own criticism of their neo-classical successors. As Joan Robinson wrote in 1948:

> In both, unemployment plays an essential part. In both, capitalism is seen as carrying within itself the seeds of its own decay. On the negative side, as against the orthodox equilibrium theory, the systems of Keynes and Marx stand together, and there is now, for the first time, enough common ground between Marxist and academic economists to make discussion possible. In spite of this there has still been very little serious study of Marx by English academic economists.

Some, no doubt, were deterred by his stylistic opacity. Although Robinson herself thought that Marx's theory of crises in Volume II of *Das Kapital* had close affinities with Keynes, she confessed that 'I may have overemphasized the resemblance. The last two volumes of *Capital*... are excessively obscure and have been subjected to many interpretations. The waters are dark and it may be that whoever peers into them sees his own face.'

But the principal reason for ignoring the link between Marx and Keynes – indeed for neglecting Marx altogether – was probably political. Keynes himself was a Liberal rather than a socialist, who proudly declared that 'the class war will find me on the side of the educated bourgeoisie', and Keynesianism became the new orthodoxy for Western economists and politicians in the mid-twentieth century – at precisely the time when the Cold War made Marx's name synonymous with the enemy. Few non-Marxists wished to be tainted by association.

The great exception was the Austrian-born economist Joseph Schumpeter. Capitalism has had no more zealous champion than Schumpeter, who remains a hero for many American entrepreneurs, yet his famous work *Capitalism, Socialism and Democracy* (1942) begins with a 54-page assessment of Marx's achievements which is as unexpectedly generous as Marx's own tributes to the bourgeoisie in the *Communist Manifesto.* As a prophet, he admits, Marx suffered from 'wrong vision and faulty analysis', particularly in his prediction of increasing misery for the workers. Nevertheless, 'Marx saw [the] process of industrial change more clearly and he realized its pivotal importance more fully than any other economist of his time', thus becoming 'the first economist of top rank to see and to teach systematically how economic theory may be turned into historical analysis and how the historical narrative may be turned into *histoire raisonnée*'. A few pages later he poses the question 'Can capitalism survive?' and replies: 'No. I do not think it can.' This may seem a bizarre comment in a book designed as a robust defence of the entrepreneurial spirit, and certainly Schumpeter – unlike Marx – took no pleasure in it. ('If a doctor predicts that his patient will die presently, this does not mean that he desires it.') His point was that capitalist innovation – new products, new methods of producing them – was a force of 'creative destruction' which might ultimately become too successful, and therefore too destructive, for its own good.

By the last decade of the twentieth century the sibylline warnings of both Schumpeter and Marx seemed to have been confounded. With Communism in its death throes, liberal American-style capitalism could now reign unchallenged – perhaps for ever. 'What we are witnessing,' Francis Fukuyama proclaimed in 1989, 'is not just the end of the Cold War, or a passing of a particular period of postwar history, but the end of history as such: that is, the end point of mankind's ideological evolution.' But history soon returned with a vengeance. By August 1998, economic meltdown in Russia, currency collapses in Asia and market panic around the world prompted the *Financial Times* to wonder if we had moved 'from the triumph of global capitalism to its crisis in barely a decade'. The article was headlined '*Das Kapital* Revisited'.

Even those who gained most from the system began to question its viability. George Soros, the billionaire speculator who had been blamed for both the Asian and the Russian debacles, warned in *The Crisis of Global Capitalism: Open Society Endangered* (1998) that the herd instinct of capital-owners must be controlled before they trampled everyone else underfoot:

> The capitalist system by itself shows no tendency toward equilibrium. The owners of capital seek to maximize their profits. Left to their own devices, they would continue to accumulate capital until the situation became unbalanced. Marx and Engels gave a very good analysis of the capitalist

system 150 years ago, better in some ways, I must say, than the equilibrium theory of classical economics… The main reason why their dire predictions did not come true was because of countervailing political interventions in democratic countries. Unfortunately we are once again in danger of drawing the wrong conclusions from the lessons of history. This time the danger comes not from communism but from market fundamentalism.

During the Cold War, when the Communist states venerated Marx's work as holy writ – complete and infallible – those on the other side of the struggle reviled him as an agent of the devil. With the toppling of the Berlin Wall, however, he acquired new admirers in the unlikeliest places. 'We should not be too quick to congratulate ourselves on the defeat of Marx, along with Marxism,' the right-wing economist Jude Wanniski wrote in 1994. 'Our world society is much more fluid than it was in his day, but the process of renewal is not guaranteed. The forces of reaction that he correctly identified have to be conquered by each succeeding generation, a monumental task that now faces ours.' Wanniski, who coined the phrase 'supply-side economics', cited *Das Kapital* as the main inspiration for his theory that production rather than demand was the key to prosperity. As a supporter of free trade and the gold standard, an enemy of bureaucracy and an admirer of the Klondike spirit, Marx was 'one of the titans of classical theory and practice' – and a seer of genius as well. He came 'extremely close to the truth' in his suggestion that capitalism sowed the seeds of its own destruction: 'That is, if capitalism requires relentless competition, yet capitalists are doing everything they can do to destroy competition, we have a system that is inherently unsustainable – as with animals who devour their young.'

In October 1997 the economics correspondent of the *New Yorker*, John Cassidy, reported a conversation with a British investment banker working in New York. 'The longer I spend on Wall Street,' the banker said, 'the more convinced I am that Marx was right. There is a Nobel Prize out there for an economist who resurrects Marx and puts it into a coherent theory. I am absolutely convinced that Marx's approach is the best way to look at capitalism.' His curiosity aroused, Cassidy read Marx for the first time and decided that his friend was right. He found 'riveting passages about globalization, inequality, political corruption, monopolization, technical progress, the decline of high culture, and the enervating nature of modern existence – issues that economists are now confronting anew, sometimes without realizing that they are walking in Marx's footsteps'. Quoting the famous slogan coined by James Carville for Bill Clinton's presidential campaign in 1992 ('It's the economy, stupid'), Cassidy pointed out that 'Marx's own term for this theory was "the materialist conception of history", and it is now so widely accepted that analysts of all political views use it, like Carville, without any attribution. When conservatives argue that the welfare state is doomed because it stifles private enterprise, or that the Soviet Union collapsed because it could not match the efficiency of Western capitalism, they are adopting Marx's argument that economics is the driving force of human development.'

Like Molière's bourgeois gentleman, who discovered to his amazement that for more than forty years he had been speaking prose without knowing it, much of the Western bourgeoisie had absorbed Marx's ideas without ever noticing. It was a belated reading of Marx in the 1990s that inspired the financial journalist James Buchan to write his brilliant study, *Frozen Desire: an inquiry into the meaning of money* (1997). As Buchan explained:

> Marx is so embedded in our Western cast of thought that few people are even aware of their debt to him. Everybody I know now believes that their attitudes are to an extent a creation of their material circumstances – 'that, on the contrary, their social being determines their consciousness', as Marx wrote – and that changes in the ways things are produced profoundly affect the affairs of humanity even outside the workshop or factory.
>
> It is largely through Marx, rather than political economy, that those notions have come down to us. Equally, everybody I know has a feeling that history is not just one damn thing after another… but is a sort of process in which something human – Liberty? Happiness? Human Potential? Something nice, anyway – becomes progressively actual. Marx didn't originate the feeling, but he made it current.

Even the *Economist* journalists John Micklethwait and Adrian Wooldridge, eager cheerleaders for turbo-capitalism, acknowledged the debt. 'As a prophet of socialism Marx may be kaput,' they wrote in *A Future Perfect: The Challenge and Hidden Promise of Globalization* (2000), 'but as a prophet of the "universal interdependence of nations" as he called globalization, he can still seem startlingly relevant... his description of globalization remains as sharp today as it was 150 years ago.' Their greatest fear was that 'the more successful globalization becomes the more it seems to whip up its own backlash' – that, in other words, Marx might have been right to suggest that 'the development of modern industry... cuts from under its feet the very foundation on which the bourgeoisie produces and appropriates products. What the bourgeoisie therefore produces, above all, are its own grave-diggers.' For all their triumphalism, Micklethwait and Wooldridge had an uneasy suspicion that the creative destruction wrought by global capitalism 'may have a natural stall point, a moment when people can take no more'.

The fall of the bourgeoisie and the victory of the proletariat have not come to pass. But Marx's errors or unfulfilled prophecies about capitalism are eclipsed and transcended by the piercing accuracy with which he revealed the nature of the beast. While all that is solid still melts into air, *Das Kapital*'s vivid portrayal of the forces that govern our lives – and of the instability, alienation and exploitation they produce – will never lose its resonance, or its power to bring the world into focus. As that *New Yorker* article concluded in 1997:

'His books will be worth reading as long as capitalism endures.' Far from being buried under the rubble of the Berlin Wall, Marx may only now be emerging in his true significance. He could yet become the most influential thinker of the twenty-first century.

INDEX

Index compiled by Meg Davies
(Registered Indexer, Society of Indexers)